Help!
My Dog Has
An Attitude

Gwen Bohnenkamp

D1053590

Help!
My Dog Has An Attitude
(Prevention and Treatment of
Temperament Problems in the Pet Dog)

Perfect Paws, Inc.
PO Box 717 Belmont, CA 94002
415-595-1962

copyright © 1994
by Gwen Bohnenkamp
Library of Congress
ISBN 05935864
BNB Publishing
Printed in the USA

Contents

About the author

Gwen Bohnenkamp, an internationally recognized author and behaviorist, has been training dogs for over 15 years. She is President of Perfect Paws, Inc. of San Francisco, providing training and consultation services to pet owners, veterinarians and humane associations throughout the United States and Canada. As Vice President of The Center for Applied Animal Behavior in Berkeley California, she co-authored a series of behavior booklets and the Sirius training video with veterinarian Ian Dunbar. At the San Francisco SPCA, Gwen founded and directed the largest and most comprehensive animal behavior correction program in the United States. She established and implemented the San Francisco SPCA's Animal Behavior Hotline, the country's first call-in animal behavior correction service. Gwen has spoken on the topic of animal behavior for numerous civic and professional organizations, including the *Commonwealth Club of California.* She writes for various publications and publishes her own newsletter, Behavior Headlines. Gwen has appeared in a variety of media including TV (where she had her own segment titled "Pet Calls"), newspaper and magazine (People Magazine, Ladies Home Journal, Better Homes and Gardens, TV Guide); and for over eight years has been on Northern California's most popular news-talk radio station, answering questions on animal behavior. She instructs a university course on Applied Animal Behavior; is a California Superior Court qualified canine behavior expert; and is the author of *Manners for the Modern Dog; Manners for the Modern Dog-Revised & Expanded; From the Cat's Point of View;* and *Kitty Kassettes.*

For
Bosco, Brandy, Naomi,
Ricci, Maggie, Sophie and Pal

Special Thanks to:
My husband, John;
My father, Larry Vidinha;
Gary Collings; JoAnn Knecht
and Debra Finucane

Cover Design and Art Direction by
Robert Eames

Illustrations by Matthew Dong

MIRROR, MIRROR ON THE WALL, WHAT IS WRONG WITH MY DOG?

Chapter 1

There are really only two reasons why dogs bark, leap, lunge, growl, snarl, snap, fight with other dogs, kill cats, dislike children and bite. The same two reasons explain why dogs are fearful, shy or neurotic. A handful are born that way. The rest are made that way by "we the people."

Naturally, one doesn't get a dog with the clear intent that three years later it would bite the face of the child next door. One doesn't pick out a new dog consciously thinking, "Oh goody, goody, now I can start training this dog to be fearful and aggressive."

Obviously we don't consciously and intentionally train our dogs to be this way. So how, why and where do things go wrong? And what can we do to prevent or correct it?

The average dog owner has the attitude, "If there isn't a problem, why bother?" That's a big mistake. We spend more time and money making sure nothing goes wrong with our car than we do making sure nothing goes wrong with our dog. We know it is simpler, cheaper and easier to change the oil in our car regularly, rather than to wait until the motor breaks down before doing anything. It's easier to never start smoking in the first place than to hope that the doctors will cure our lung cancer. But with dogs, we don't realize that it is infinitely easier to prevent problems than it is to cure them. It's much better to anticipate problems and head them off, rather than to wait to see if they occur, then try to fix them.

Unfortunately, many owners do not recognize that their dog has a problem until tragedy strikes. This is really a shame because problem behavior is so easily preventable and highly predictable. I have seen dogs chomp down, and blood spurt out of the hands and arms of owners, yet the owners will not admit that their dog just bit them. They make excuses for the dog. "Oh, the dog was just teething." "He didn't mean it." "It was just a love nip." "I don't mind a little mouthing." Owners dismiss their dog's biting as teething, chewing, mouthing, nibbling or love-nipping. What they may call "mouthing" can just as easily be called "biting" or "an attack" if the victim is a young child whose mother hates dogs.

Most people have the illusion that their dog would never dream of biting them. They are so stunned and shocked when their dog does bite that they continue to make all kinds of excuses. Here's a few typical ones:

I took him by surprise because it was dark in the house.
The dog's hearing must be going because he's never
bitten before.
The dog must be cranky today because I left her alone
all day yesterday.
The dog mistook me for the cat.
The dog was just overly excited.
The dog doesn't like children.
The dog doesn't like women.
The dog doesn't like people in uniforms.
The dog is angry or upset.
The dog is jealous.
The dog is hungry.
The dog didn't get his regular walk today.
The dog is - fill in the blank.

Many people will acknowledge that their dog is
possessive or territorial but they don't consider it a
problem. "Oh yes, of course my dog will growl and
snap at anyone who tries to take his bone, but he's not
aggressive." Even after the dog has bitten, people deny
that they have a problem. As long as no one crosses the
dog or tries to take anything away from him, there is no
problem. Some people walk around their own home as
if tip-toeing on eggshells in an effort not to provoke the
dog, out of fear of being bitten. But ask them if their
dog has an aggression problem and the answer is "no."

Too many dog owners wait until they are faced with a lawsuit, plastic surgery bills and the loss of their homeowners insurance before they recognize they have a problem and before they are willing to do anything about it.

I received a call recently from a person whose dog bit a neighbor's child. The day after the bite, the father of the child came out with a baseball bat and hit the dog in the face. The child is in the hospital, the dog is at the vet, lawsuits and charges of cruelty are flying back and forth. The dog's owner called me for advice. They said their dog never liked children and had always growled at kids, but they never thought he would actually bite one.

To make matters worse, if and when owners do acknowledge a problem and seek help, they often get bad advice. The advice ranges from ridiculous and unrealistic to downright cruel or dangerous.

The standard but faulty remedy for aggression is aggression. "Fill an empty soda can with rocks and smack the dog under the chin with it. Be sure it's under the chin so the dog won't see it coming. That way the dog won't know you hit him and won't become afraid of you." What a crock of baloney! Do these people really think dogs are dumb and blind to boot? Most dogs who are struck with objects inevitably end up biting the bearer of these objects. This advice is inhumane and dangerous.

Another favorite bit of advice that many people are given: "Put a choke chain on the dog and hang him until he goes unconscious." This is downright cruel. Dogs treated this way become excessively hand-shy and will bite anyone who reaches for them.

A commonly accepted but erroneous solution to aggression is the "alpha roll over" (throw the dog on his back, hold him down and growl at his throat). This is just plain ludicrous. If you own a large dog, why not walk in front of a speeding truck instead? If you own a little dog, then spare the trouble and just shove your hand in a meat grinder. In other words, the results to you will most likely be the same. Just imagine trying to grab a snarling, lunging, aggressive 90 pound dog, throwing him on his back and then holding him down. Small dogs can move at the speed of light. Before you could even touch this dog to grab him, your hands could look like hamburger. I've seen it. Ask any plastic surgeon who reconstructs the faces of dog bite victims and they will also tell you the results are the same.

Bad advice abounds. Be careful. Here are the ten most frequent one-shot cures for aggression that you will be told to do (even by alleged experts). Anyone who employs these methods ends up with a dog that still bites or who has other major behavior problems.

Bad / Wrong Advice
that You Will Hear or Read:

1. Hit, kick or slap the dog, especially on his nose or under his chin.
2. Twist or pinch the dog's ear until he yelps.
3. Use some device like a newspaper, fly swatter, stick or empty soda can or bottle (instead of your hands) to strike the dog.
4. Cram your hand into the dog's mouth or down his throat.
5. Stab the roof of the dog's mouth with your fingernail or pinch his tongue.
6. Grab the dog by the scruff and shake.
7. Bite the dog.
8. Hang the dog by his neck.
9. Isolate the dog, often called "time-out."
10. Alpha roll the dog.

If you do any of the above, you will most likely cause bigger problems in your dog.

Dogs growl, snarl, snap and bite for many reasons. There is no such thing as an unprovoked bite. Just because we are unable to determine the reason does not mean there is none. There are as many reasons for bites as there are victims of bites. This book will address the most common temperament and aggression problems in the pet dog. And it will provide you with humane and effective methods of prevention and treatment.

The Greatest Cause of Aggression - A Killer Attitude

We have a misconception that an aggressive dog constantly goes around snarling, threatening and attacking everything and everyone in sight. Quite the contrary, aggressive dogs are usually good natured 99% of the time. Very rarely does a dog change overnight from being trustworthy to aggressive. The seeds of aggression are already there. They were planted during puppyhood. Unfortunately, it is usually we the owners who unintentionally create a fearful or aggressive dog.

When we bring home our new puppy, it's so easy to forget that this adorable, precious little furball is an animal - a dog - with its own set of species-specific behaviors and instincts. It doesn't even occur to us that as a canine, it is entirely different from us. Dogs have their own set of customs, rituals, needs, desires, habits, thoughts and emotions. They are different from us genetically, physically, emotionally and socially. They have a different means of communication than we do. By not truly understanding their nature, we superimpose our standards on them. In other words, we assume that what makes us happy will make them happy. We erroneously assume that what makes us sad will make them sad. We think that what we want, they want.

Dogs still operate on a survival level. Their needs are not as complex as ours. They are not motivated politically, environmentally, economically or religiously. They really have no morality or ethics as we know morality and ethics. They do not steal from the trash can because they are immoral and have no values or respect for the property of others. They do not steal trash as a premeditated act of revenge for something you have done or failed to do. They steal trash because it is pleasurable, rewarding and advantageous. They may or may not even be hungry.

Dogs live in the moment. If you come home and find the trash scattered around the kitchen and you scold the dog, he may act ashamed, guilty, horrified and repentant, but he is not. His actions are a survival mechanism. In the dog's world, this behavior is an effective means of warding off an attack by another dog. And it works - with dogs. When his "I'm just a worthless worm, don't attack me" gestures do not succeed in stopping your aggressive behavior, the dog becomes confused, insecure and stressed. Your dog may know you are angry about the trash, but what about it? Are you angry because the trash is scattered in the wrong place? Are you angry because that trash was reserved for someone else to scatter around? Is the mess not messy enough? Dogs live in the moment and any delayed reprimands or punishments by you erode your dog's trust and confidence in you.

The only way to let the dog know that you are unhappy when he tips over the trash is to catch him in the act and scold him. But still, the only thing you are effectively teaching the dog is to not get caught. As far as he is concerned, getting in the trash is not a bad thing. The bad thing is getting caught by you. So if you are out of the house, guess who is going to get into the trash again? Stealing trash is not an issue of morality for dogs. The issue is what is beneficial at the moment. Getting the trash is beneficial. Getting caught is not beneficial. Result: Dog steals trash when he knows he won't be caught. Owners show their lack of understanding of dog behavior when they claim, "He knows he's been bad." The only thing the dog knows is that you will be or you are angry. Video tape the dog getting into the trash when you are not home. You will see no shame, evil smirks or signs of guilt. The guilty looks only appear when you appear.

Since punishment after-the-fact does no good and reprimand in-the-act has limited value, what's an owner to do? Put the trash where the dog cannot get to it. When you are not home to supervise your dog, do not allow him freedom to get into trouble. If you come home and find a mess, simply clean it up. Do not leave temptations out for the dog to get into next time.

Most of us acquire a dog for emotional reasons - love, companionship, security, etc. and we tend to become emotionally involved to the dog's detriment. A unique characteristic of the dog is its unconditional love. Sadly, even abused dogs love their owners. They may be neurotic but they love their owner. We don't need to work on gaining our dog's love. What we need to work on gaining is our dog's trust, respect and confidence. In an attempt to return the unconditional love the dog gives us, we tend to over-coddle them.

Over-coddling a puppy is the greatest cause of temperament problems. Instead of growing up to be a well-adjusted, happy and secure dog, the over-coddled pup grows up to be skittish, untrusting, anxious and neurotic. Over-coddling causes a dog to be afraid of or aggressive towards other dogs and people. Over-coddling prevents the puppy from developing normal social canine behavior. This erupts into unacceptable behavior later on. We create an assortment of problems that could so easily have been prevented by not over-coddling the puppy during her critical developmental period.

What is Over-Coddling?

We are so afraid that our puppy will break, as if she is constructed of the finest, thinnest crystal, that we touch and handle her as if she were a fragile ornament. We are so afraid that our puppy will be hurt or traumatized that we shelter her from everything. If our parents treated us like we treat our puppy, we would never learn to ride a bicycle because our knees might be skinned. We would never have any friends because other children might hurt our feelings.

No one is allowed to make any loud or sudden noises around the puppy because it might upset her. Don't touch or pick the puppy up when she doesn't want to be bothered. Don't disturb her while she is sleeping, eating or chewing on her toys. Don't take her outside, it's raining. Don't let the puppy pick up anything on the ground, it might be bad for her. Don't let the puppy around children, because they are too rough and rambunctious. She might get hurt. Don't leave her alone when she is whining. Be sure to pick her up and soothe her. We don't want the puppy to feel abandoned!

We are so afraid that our puppy's feelings will be bruised. After all, the puppy is so cute and innocent. We haven't the heart to reprimand obnoxious behavior. We assume that her biting, leaping, ripping at our clothes, mounting and biting the kids is just a phase that she will out-grow. But the dog will continue to bite and use us as a spring board for one reason only: We allow it. We rationalize that our dog isn't really trying to hurt us, he's just being friendly. He's playing. We fear that if we tell him not to bite, then maybe he won't love us anymore. We don't want to take any chances that we might lose this unconditional love. We won't stop the biting because we are afraid of hurting the dog's feelings at a time when he is happy. We are worried that we might break the dog's spirit.

Owners can be so paranoid about possibly breaking their dog's spirit. One doesn't break a dog's spirit by teaching her some socially-acceptable manners. You break a dog's spirit by being inconsistent, untrustworthy, unpredictable, abusive, and by not allowing the dog to be fulfilled as a dog. You break a dog's spirit by trying to treat her like a helpless human infant. She has a canine spirit, not a human spirit. If you

follow the guidelines in this book you will never break
your dog's spirit. Instead you will bring her spirit alive,
give her energy, help her thrive and be fulfilled.

The over-emotional, over-protective, over-indulgent,
don't-break-the-dog's-spirit attitude (over-coddling)
usually results in an unsocialized dog who is aggressive
and fearful. This dog cannot be left alone without
barking, whining, and destroying the owner's home.
This dog cannot be trusted around children because she
will bite them. If this dog steals a chicken bone or other
dangerous item, no one will be able to take it away
from her. This dog will probably grow up eating
inedible items such as clothing, rocks, plastic and
paper. This dog's owner will have huge veterinary bills
when the dog becomes sick from ingesting these items.
This dog may become a finicky eater and will have to
have special foods cooked for her. The owner will have
a difficult time finding anyone willing to groom this
dog. She will have to be muzzled for a simple
vaccination or bath. She will have to be muzzled to
have her nails clipped. This dog will never be able to be
off-leash with other dogs. If it's raining outside this dog
will soil the house because she will refuse to go out in
the rain to do her business. These owners have doomed
their dogs and themselves to a miserable existence.

Many owners will not put up with this misery and end up euthanizing (killing) the dog; or they give the dog away to an unsuspecting, uninformed new owner who will eventually have the dog destroyed or pass it on too.

These type of owners give dogs a bad name and force anti-dog legislation - all in the name of love. Ironic, isn't it?

Following are a few real-life examples of owners who loved their dogs to death. I will always use fictitious names to keep the owners and their dogs anonymous.

"Scampy" was a happy-go-lucky, extremely friendly, affectionate dog. She loved people and demonstrated it by gleefully jumping on everyone. The owner did not want to train her to stop doing this because he was so afraid he might break her spirit. She was 8 months old when she jumped on a frail, elderly man. He tumbled over, was knocked unconscious and his hip was shattered. The emergency paramedics were called and the man was carried off in an ambulance. He had no insurance. Naturally a lawsuit was filed and the dog owner lost. The dog owner almost lost his home and did lose his dog. With that history he has not been able to find any insurance company that will cover him as long as he has a dog. His choice now is own a dog or own a home.

"Max" was an intelligent, handsome dog. He was willing to learn and please. The problem was he received no instruction. During training, the owner felt that she was being cruel by making Max stay when he really wanted to play with the other dogs. She refused to train him to stay. One day she opened the front door and told him to "stay." This really baffles me; first she refuses to teach him to stay and then she gives him the command as if he knew what it meant! Of course the dog didn't stay, what did she expect? Instead, he bolted into the street, was hit by a bus and killed. She broke his spirit all right, by not training him. Dead dogs exhibit no spirit.

"Ulysses" started class as an energetic, friendly puppy of 4 months. He was the boyfriend's dog living at the girlfriend's house. He took to training immediately and performed well. Infatuated and thrilled with having a new puppy, everyone wanted to play with the dog; no one wanted to be the "bad" guy by imposing rules and guidelines. The boyfriend worked days, the girlfriend worked nights. It seemed to be the perfect setup for the dog. Ulysses would never be left alone. Soon the novelty wore off. In one month the dog had doubled in size and the girlfriend was unable to handle him anymore. The boyfriend is able to handle the dog but doesn't have the time. The dog is running amok in the house, knocking over furniture and jumping on guests.

His little puddles that were previously tolerated became pools and lakes. So he is put outside and left there. Anytime the girlfriend tried to go outside, the dog jumped up and mouthed her. He was just happy to see her. He didn't mean any harm. But she decided she had had enough, so she stopped doing anything for him at all. When the boyfriend tried to train or walk the dog, he felt he could control the dog by yelling and hitting him. Walking was unpleasant so he decided to let the dog run off-leash in a dog park. Since Ulysses was not socialized with other dogs, he acted either fearful or aggressive towards them. Ulysses did not know how to play. Because Ulysses was too difficult to walk on-leash and too untrustworthy off-leash, the owner stopped taking him out altogether. So Ulysses lives his entire life in a back yard with no social contact. Basically he is only given food and water and is otherwise totally isolated. The couple feel too guilty to give the dog away. This dog is a time bomb, ready to explode. When it does explode, Ulysses will be euthanized. In the mean time, he has a miserable existence.

These people took a perfectly normal, wonderful dog and turned him into an aggressive, asocial, fearful animal. How did it happen? They saw a cute puppy and in an emotional moment, couldn't live without him. They didn't realize how important is was to train him.

They never understood the idea of socialization and that a puppy needs to get around other dogs while it is young so it would learn how to play. Isolating the dog in the back yard arrested his social development. He is now unfriendly not only to other dogs but to people as well. Even if they are now willing to do the right thing, this dog will never be what he could have been. They didn't accept the importance of puppyhood. This is time you can't buy back. Don't blow it for your puppy, give him the best start possible. If you've already blown it, start making amends immediately.

When working on any problem, but especially biting, fearful or aggressive behavior, consistency is extremely important. For success, you need both the dog's trust and respect. Trust and respect go hand in hand. If you have one and not the other, you will confuse your dog and your problems will not be resolved. Training your dog is never a one-shot deal. It needs constant maintenance or it will deteriorate.

SOCIALIZATION

Chapter 2

If you've decided you don't want to create a canine monster, what's the first step? Begin by imagining what kind of dog you would like to have. How about a dog that is well-adjusted? One that you can trust around people, other dogs and even cats. One that respects you, trusts you and is loyal to you and your family. How about a dog that will sit to greet company instead of barrel them over? How about a dog that you can handle easily while giving him a bath or taking him to the vet? Wouldn't it be nice to have a dog you can trust never to growl or bite your children? Think of your own lifestyle and what is important to you, then use these principles of socialization to give your puppy or dog the best life possible.

Prevention - Puppies

If you don't want your dog to do certain things as an adult, don't let your puppy do them. It's cute and relatively harmless when a ten pound puppy runs across the room and jumps up on you, but think about what it's going to feel like when he is 65 pounds. Even dogs that will weigh no more than 12 pounds as an adult can be a nuisance, leaping about your ankles and knees with sharp claws or muddy feet. If you don't want your adult dog biting your hands and ripping your clothes, don't let him do it as a puppy. If you don't want your adult dog to run amok in your house, don't let him do it as a puppy. Your puppy's first experiences and habits will stay with him for a life time. It's easier to prevent habits from forming by simply not allowing the puppy to do certain things than it will be to change his behavior after it becomes an ingrained habit.

The majority of problems that adult dogs have is a result of what their owner did <u>not</u> do when he was a puppy. Puppies go through a critical developmental period between 8 and 18 weeks of age. Whatever you want your dog to be socialized with as an adult, he must be introduced to as a puppy. The biggest mistake people make is that they don't start socializing their pup until this critical developmental stage has passed. Sheltering your puppy past the socialization period is equivalent to locking a human child in a closet until he or she is between 9 and 12 years of age. If we treated our children like we treated our puppies, they would never learn to have fun because they might get hurt. Don't go camping, the child may be bitten by a mosquito or god-forbid, a bee! No sports, that's too dangerous. No swimming, no skating, no bike riding, no Jungle-Gym. They would never have any friends or develop social skills.

If a dog is not socialized with something, he will react badly to it. He will hide from it; cower and become unreasonably anxious; bolt away from it; bite it if it approaches; or attack it in an effort to keep it away. Think of everything you want your dog to be comfortable with and expose these things to your puppy during this stage. If you do not want your dog to be afraid of loud noises, then don't shelter him as a puppy from loud noises. If you don't want your dog to be afraid of the rain, don't shelter him as a puppy from the rain. If you don't want your dog to chase and kill cats, then socialize your puppy with cats. If you do not want your dog to fear or dislike children, then your puppy must be socialized with children. Almost every dog that has ever bitten a child is a dog that was not properly socialized with children and the things children do.

Socialization does not mean you swing to the opposite extreme of over-protection and become irresponsible. Yes, your dog must be socialized, but with some common sense. Don't drop the dog off on the street and say, "Get used to cars, buddy, I'll be back in an hour." Socialization means providing your puppy with the safe opportunity to explore and experience things on his own while you monitor and supervise.

Many people erroneously presume they have socialized their dog because they invited a couple of friends over to the house. Just because the puppy has met and become friendly with a few other people doesn't mean he will be relaxed around strangers. Just because your puppy plays with the dog next door doesn't mean he will be relaxed when meeting strange dogs. Just because you take your puppy to your friend's house doesn't mean he will be relaxed in all new environments. It's important to provide your puppy with the opportunity to experience a wide variety of circumstances , especially situations that you expect the dog to regularly encounter during his life. If you live in the country and occasionally want to take your dog to the city, be sure to take him there as a puppy. If not, your dog will be fearful of the busy, noisy environment of the city.

Socialization is a continual process. Many owners give their puppies an excellent start, then assuming the pup to be adequately socialized, they suddenly and abruptly stop. The pup was given one month of socialization, then returned to a life of isolation. It won't be long before this pup will begin to become wary and suspicious of strangers, and non-routine situations or circumstances.

Children

Since children are the biggest victims of dog bites, it's critical that you socialize your pup with kids, lest you and your dog become another statistic. Don't assume that just because you have a child or two in your house that this is sufficient. It's critical to socialize your puppy with children of different ages. There is a tremendous difference between a child of six months, two years, five years and nine years. A dog that is comfortable around a nine year old will not necessarily be comfortable around a two year old.

When it comes to socializing your puppy with children, time is wasting. Dogs already have a bad reputation when it comes to kids and the clock is working against you. It's extremely easy to socialize a tiny, fluffy, cute puppy with children. Everyone loves a puppy. When I start the child-socialization process, I have mothers and children rushing towards me to look at and pet the puppy. A very young pup is not perceived as a dog yet, and therefore not a threat. Rarely is anyone afraid of a very young pup. If I were to wait just one month, the little puppy is twice the size and looking more and more like a dog. Instead of mothers and children flocking over to see the puppy, they ignore us or turn the other way. The novelty and cuteness of puppyness is no longer there. Now people shrug their shoulder and think, "Oh just another dog."

Some mothers will even grab their children and cross the street, afraid to take any chances with a dog.

A young puppy is also much easier to control around children. Most people cannot control their six month old dog when a leaf blows by, much less around a group of shrieking children. If you want your dog to be friendly with children, it must happen as a puppy. Period. There's no other time to realistically accomplish this.

Let's say you're intent on child-socializing your menacing looking, 85 pound, nine month old dog. What do you need to accomplish this? Children! How many mothers are going to donate their three year olds to your cause? Zero. Get the picture? It can't be done. So if you don't do it while your dog is a puppy, forget it. Time is wasting. You need to socialize your puppy with children yesterday.

Etc.

You name it - if you don't want your dog to fear it or dislike it, then you must socialize your dog to it while he is a puppy. If your adult dog chases and kills cats, again, where are you going to get the cats to socialize your dog? What about horses? Joggers? Bicyclists? Softball games? Parties? Picnics? Buses? Shopping carts? You name it . . . just do it.

Don't wait until your dog is five months old to introduce him to grooming and bathing. It can be a nightmare. Some dogs have an absolute fit, screaming and thrashing uncontrollably when simply having their toenails clipped. It's impossible to cut a nail when you can't hold the paw still. It's unbelievable how many dogs have to be muzzled and held down by an army of people for this event. Large dogs have to be anesthetized. This is truly ridiculous.

All it takes is some time and energy on your part when the dog is a young puppy to get it used to these things. You must let your puppy get used to having his feet and nails touched while he is small enough for you to handle him. You must get your dog accustomed to being bathed, brushed and groomed while he is a young puppy.

If your dog needs special grooming and clipping, introduce him to the routine and equipment early. Take your puppy to visit the groomer long before he actually needs clipping. The noise and activity of a grooming facility can be frightening to a dog. Be sure your dog is accustomed to the buzzing noises of shavers and clippers, the splashing noises of running water, the humming of blow dryers, the barking of other dogs and the general environment of the grooming process and facility. Be sure your dog's first visit is a rewarding, pleasurable experience.

Now or Never

Early experience has a tremendous and lasting impact on your dog's behavior. The key is to capitalize on the dog's critical socialization period. Once this period is passed, you will never get it back. There is not a lot you need to do other than provide your pup with the opportunity to experience life and see things for himself. Don't interfere with his learning process. New things can startle any dog. If you react by laughing, giggling, rushing in to soothe and protect, your puppy will be rewarded for his shy or fearful behavior. He will assume that acting nervous, skittish or anxious is the appropriate response because you are apparently so approving of it.

Precedents and
Socializing the Fearful or Adult Dog

If you just brought a new adult dog into your home, she will usually be on her best behavior for a few weeks. During this time she is evaluating and assessing the new environment. Once the dog begins to feel secure, she will begin to test the waters to see what latitude she has. Dogs are especially sensitive and impressionable when in a new and unfamiliar setting. Each experience she has now will leave a permanent impression.

Any effort you put into training at this time will have a long-lasting effect. But likewise, anything you allow your dog to do during this time will set a precedent that will be difficult to change. It's easy for new owners to spoil and indulge their newly acquired canine companion. Guard against this.

If your long time pal, or your new buddy was not socialized as a puppy, then begin the process immediately. However, as a word of caution, please be careful and considerate not only of your dog but of other people and their dogs as well. If you do have the 85 pound dog who dislikes children, it is not safe to try to socialize the dog with kids. It's far too risky. If your dog likes to attack cats, please don't attempt to socialize your dog with them. The best you can do in these types of circumstances is to prevent any unfortunate incidents.

Following are examples of how to socialize the dog or puppy who is already fearful. Every dog will be leery of different things, so approach each situation slowly and meticulously. Use the same principles presented in whatever situation or circumstance you need it.

Let's take an example of a dog who is terrified of baths. If you use this method with a fearful, young puppy, you can reach your desired goal in a matter of weeks. With most adult dogs, it will take a minimum of six to nine months and sometimes even longer. There will be some dogs who will never like baths no matter what you do. But it is certainly worth a try.

Several times a day, place the dog in an empty tub. Show him that the tub is a fun place to be. Play with him, give him special treats, massage him, do anything that the dog likes while he is just sitting or standing in an empty tub. You can speed the process by withholding affection, attention and treats at all other times. Some dogs catch on so quickly that they deliberately jump into the tub just so they can collect on the goodies.

When the dog shows no hesitation at being picked up and placed in the tub, then run the water. Don't try to get him wet until he shows no signs of fear from the running water. Again, make this a fun event. The next step would be to get the dog wet, that's all. When it's not a big deal for the dog to be placed in the tub and wetted down, then massage the wet dog without any shampoo. When the dog is comfortable with this, then it will be time to go ahead and soap up. At this stage, just soap up and wash the legs or feet. When the dog is relaxed with this stage, then on subsequent baths, wash only his back or chest, and so on. It's important to keep the baths relatively short, so it's over with quickly. Gradually get the dog used to longer baths that cover more and more of his body. Keep your own attitude relaxed, happy, fun and patient. If you become stressed or impatient, you can set the entire process back several months. If you try to proceed too quickly, you will not give the dog enough time to overcome his fears and this too will result in failure.

Never forget: It is better to go too slowly and succeed, than to hurry and fail.

Don't forget the dryer. Most dogs do not take readily to a blow dryer. Introduce it the same way - slowly. From the beginning, run the blow dryer at some distance away from the dog. Do this until the dog shows no signs of fear. You can speed the process up by rewarding the dog with praise and treats whenever he acts calm and relaxed. When the dog is not afraid of the noise, then quickly run the warm air across his body for no more than two seconds. The next time, make it three seconds and so on. Be sure your dog is not afraid of the dryer long before you actually use it to dry him.

The purpose of the following exercises is to help your dog learn to accept unusual and unexpected events. With a young puppy, success can be achieved sometimes in a matter of hours. With an adult dog, it can take months to years.

Out of the blue, open an umbrella in front of your dog and set it down on the floor. Sit back and watch. There is nothing you can say or do to convince your dog that this is nothing to fear. The dog must find this out on his own. Let him run and hide, then peek out and stare at it. Usually there will be a vacillating pattern. Your dog will begin to approach, then suddenly run away. Since nothing scary happened, your dog will have the confidence to approach again, this time he may get a little closer before he runs to safety. You can accelerate the process by placing a few of the dog's favorite treats right next to or under the opened umbrella. Eventually the dog will see that the umbrella is really no different than the dining room table. It's just there. The next time you open an umbrella, the dog will probably just ignore it as if it were something as mundane as the dining room table. Try this with other unusual items or objects. Your only job is to provide the object and make sure it cannot harm the dog. The rest is up to your dog to explore and experience at his own pace.

On subsequent sessions, provide other novel stimuli or work with something you know the dog has a phobia of, such as the vacuum cleaner. Far too many dogs either attack this item or nervously hide from it. Instead of storing it away in the closet, let it set, unplugged in the living room for a couple of weeks so your dog gets used to seeing it. Leave a few tasty treats on or next to it to entice your dog to approach and investigate. Turn it on several times a day for just a few seconds so the dog gets used to its sound.

Increase the length of time you have it running. Push it around the room unplugged to be sure the dog is not afraid of it when it moves. Then push it around just a little when it is turned on. Don't push it towards the dog, always push it away at first. We don't want the dog to think that this noisy monster is on the attack.

Musical instruments or other sound producing things can be treated similarly. The first time I strummed my guitar in front of my pup, she shrieked and bolted out of the room. After about 30 seconds of dissonant strumming, she relaxed as if she couldn't even hear it. Think of things you will have and do around your home and let your dog experience them.

Phobias

Many dogs have phobias of different items or situations. To help your dog overcome them takes a tremendous amount of patience on your part. Never become discouraged or angry at what seems to be lack of progress. Some people have phobias and go through psychotherapy and counseling for years and make little progress. Some people are in therapy for a lifetime. It's reasonable that your dog too may take years to overcome a phobia.

To treat phobias, it is best to use a combination of distraction, desensitization and behavior modification.

In addition, be sure you are not unintentionally rewarding your dog for acting fearful. Do not try to soothe, calm or comfort the dog. Following are examples:

Distraction

Try to distract your dog from the stimulus that causes the fear. Brush up on her obedience training and teach her a few tricks and games. It is difficult for a dog to be frightened when she is enjoying her favorite game of fetch. Reserve a special toy that you know will get your dog excited for these occasions. It is difficult to think about the hammering noises outside when the dog is playing with her special toy or concentrating on a quick series of: come here, sit, shake hands, roll over. The idea is to distract your dog from the stimulus that causes the fear. You can then shower her with affection and attention, but for obeying your commands or for playing a game rather than for acting fearful. The key is patience and practice. Many owners complain that they have tried and failed using this method. What they did was give up too soon. If your dog is fearful of fireworks, don't wait until December 30th or July 3rd to begin teaching your dog a few tricks. Be sure she knows them well before the noisy celebrations of New Year's Eve and the Fourth of July. She will have trouble concentrating at first, so the better she knows the games, the easier it will be for her to perform them under pressure.

Desensitization

This method helps the dog overcome her fear by slowly and gradually exposing her to the stimulus that frightens her. Suppose the dog is fearful of thunder. Make a sound recording of the frightening noise and play it back to the dog while she is enjoying everyday life and activities. Some record stores have soundtracks of thunderstorms and such that you can purchase. Before starting the desensitization process, be sure to test that your dog is indeed fearful of the recorded noises when played back at full volume. After testing the recording, play it back at such a low volume that you can barely hear it, but your dog's keen senses will. This volume should produce no visible signs of stress or fear in your dog. Life should proceed as usual. Gradually, over the course of weeks or months, increase the volume in tiny increments. The volume should be increased so slowly that your dog hardly notices the change. Eventually he will be used to hearing the sounds at full volume.

If at any time, your dog shows signs of fear, decrease the volume again and proceed a little more slowly. This method will work more quickly if you combine it with distraction training as described above and behavior modification as described below. This method can be extremely time consuming. The sooner you start, the better chance you have of success.

Behavior Modification

With this method, you modify the dog's response to a stimulus. One of the most common phobias I see is hand shyness. At one level of obedience training I teach handsignals. One command begins with the owner raising an outstretched arm into the air over the dog. Inevitably, there are several dogs in class that wince, duck their head, tuck their tail and retreat. This behavior in the dog points to only one thing - the dog thinks he is about to be hit.

In this case the first thing we have to do is modify the dog's response to the hand signal so he is not afraid of this stimulus. To do this we put the dog in a down stay right in front of the owner, raise the outstretched arm and simultaneously give the dog a food treat. After about five to ten repetitions, we momentarily delay giving the treat after raising the arm. If the dog shows no wincing, the owner further delays giving the reward after raising their arm. The next step is to then raise the arm while asking the dog to sit. When the dog sits, he is immediately rewarded and praised.

With repetition, an arm reaching over the dog's head produces a quick sit rather than cowering and wincing. The dog's behavior has been modified from a fearful response to a reliable obedience response.

Help! My Dog Has An Attitude!

SOCIALIZING
WITH DOGS

Chapter 3

There are numerous reasons to socialize a dog with other dogs. It is the only process by which dogs can learn normal canine social behavior. Some of a dog's behavior is instinctive, but some behaviors must be developed and learned from other members of their own species. Owners inhibit this process by denying their dog the opportunity to socialize during its critical developmental period. If the opportunity presents itself, owners become over-protective and interfere with the learning process. Lack of socialization and improper socialization cause dogs to be fearful, shy or aggressive towards other dogs.

It's too bad that we ruin what could be a lifetime of fun and enjoyment for our dog by not allowing socialization with other dogs during its developmental period. If the dog doesn't learn to inhibit its bite, control its emotions or read canine body language, then eventually the owner will not be able to let it off-leash to interact with other dogs. They will not be able to introduce a second dog to the household. Their dog will have to stay at home when everyone else takes their dogs to picnics and outings. It's sad that a dog may never know the pleasures of being a dog. There are too many dogs out there whose owners never let them around other dogs because the dog is not social. Being around other dogs is as normal as a dog giving birth to puppies (instead of kittens), and some dogs are denied the pleasure of socializing with other dogs because they are not given the opportunity by the owner.

Another advantage to letting your dog play with other dogs is that it wears them out so they have less energy to vent on your house and belongings. Puppies have a tremendous amount of energy and curiosity. If the energy isn't relieved, the puppy will be hundreds of times more likely to be destructive. Instead of having other puppies to play with, your puppy will chew, dig and destroy your home looking for something fun and interesting to do. If the puppy tires herself out by playing with other dogs, then she won't have the energy to destroy your house and belongings. The puppy will also sleep better at night, meaning you will also sleep better at night.

Socialized puppies that frequently and regularly romp and play with other dogs are much calmer in the household setting than fearful pups. Puppies that are too fearful to play with other dogs or puppies are usually much more hyperactive and destructive at home.

Many dogs try to play with family members like littermates because they have no other dogs to play with. By allowing your dog regular play time with other dogs, this need is filled so your dog is less likely to want to treat you like another dog. Most dogs long to be dogs and to play like a dog. If you don't fill this need, they may try to fill the void themselves. Simply by allowing your puppy to play with other dogs, the amount of play biting the puppy does to you and your children will dramatically decrease.

Bite Inhibition

Bite inhibition must be learned as a puppy. Normally this is taught to the puppy by her mother, littermates and other members of the pack. Since we take the puppy away from her canine pack and social structure, we must make up for all the things she never had the chance to finish learning. To continue her social development, your puppy needs to play with other puppies and interact with already socially skilled older dogs. If you had the opportunity to observe the normal activity of a group of puppies, the mother dog and other older members of the pack, you would see how the pups learn. Typically, the rambunctious puppies roll around, playing, tumbling and occasionally getting into spats. If you could record the number of yips and yelps you would note them ever decreasing as the weeks went by. Puppies have needle-like teeth and when they play, they bite each other's legs, ears, necks, tails, anything that fits in the pup's mouth. If one of the pups bears down too hard, it hurts! The pup that is bitten lets out a loud yip that startles the biter. The puppy that is nipped too hard usually momentarily stops playing, so the biter has momentarily lost a playmate. As this goes on, the puppies eventually realize that it is their own overly eager play-biting that causes the ear piercing noise and abrupt end of the play. They teach each other to play nicely and gently. They continue to play bite, but they learn not to bear down.

Respect

If the puppy bites the mother dog or an older dog in the pack, they are instantly reprimanded. The older dog swiftly and loudly growls right in the face of the pup. Some times the older dog will pin the pup to the ground. Other dogs will gently bite and hold the muzzle of the puppy. This all happens very fast and resembles a violent volcanic eruption, but the pup is never physically harmed. She is often so frightened by the quick reaction of the adult, that she may let out a yelp of fear and even submissively urinate. The puppy has learned a valuable lesson: Don't be disrespectful of her elders. The pup will learn to approach and ask to play with a lot less abandon. The pup learns to watch her step and not barrel over an unsuspecting adult. The pups also learn that when the older dog gives them a certain look, they had better back away or they will be reprimanded. They learn to recognize that a stare, a low quiet growl or baring of teeth from the older dog means back off, knock it off, watch your step and the like.

After several lessons, the young pup rarely gets herself into trouble because she knows the rules. The puppy can still play with the other pups but she learns to play nicely. She can still play with the adult dogs, but she learns to play respectfully. The pup learns to be a socially acceptable member of the pack. If left to themselves, the puppies learn these rules from each other and other pack members. When the pup grows into an adult dog, she too will teach the new puppy members of the pack the same lessons.

Allowing your puppy to learn respect from other dogs makes your job of gaining the puppy's respect much easier. If you give in to your puppy's every whim, your pup will never learn self-control and self-discipline. Your puppy will never learn to respect you. Your relationship will be like two 5 year olds bossing each other around. Just as a child needs a caring parent, your puppy needs a leader. If the puppy has free and clear license to do anything she wants then she will have no frame of reference when you finally try to impose your rules on her. Without any leadership, your puppy will think she is the center of the universe. By allowing the mother dog or another socialized adult dog to teach your dog some manners, your pup will have a more realistic outlook on the world. Because she has experience with having to show respect, it will be much easier for the pup to transfer this concept to you as the leader.

Some of you may have the erroneous idea that in order to gain the dog's respect, you must bully and terrorize her into submission. This is not respect. Respect is not something that is forced. It is won. A dog will not respect someone she does not trust. A good leader commands respect because the leadership is predictable, consistent and trustworthy. The puppy has confidence in herself and the leader. Never hit, kick or slap your dog. This is the quickest way to ruin your status as leader. Leaders are not aggressive tyrants.

These principles of leadership will become very apparent to you once you have seen how predictable and fair canine leaders are when teaching your dog to defer to higher rank.

Socializing Puppies

The easiest way to socialize your puppy with dogs is to leave it in the hands of other puppies and socialized dogs. If your puppy acts afraid, no amount of your coaxing and talking to her is going to convince her that everything is indeed all right. This is something that your pup has to experience on her own. You can't force it. It will happen naturally if you provide the opportunity. The shy pup will watch the other puppies playing and having a good time. Eventually she will want to join in. Sometimes the other pups come over and invite the shy pup to play. In either case, the pup soon learns that there is nothing to be afraid of. As soon as she has the confidence to play, then she can start learning. If she never plays, then she will never make mistakes. If no mistakes are made, no learning occurs.

Some of you think your puppy is socialized because you have another dog in your home or the neighbor has a dog and the two of them get together daily. Your puppy does indeed learn to interact successfully with this dog but she is a long way from being socialized. Just because you can successfully give a speech in front of your family or a friend doesn't mean you can suddenly stand up before 100 people you don't know and be relaxed giving the same speech. Living with another dog does not constitute socialization.

Others of you think your puppy has been socialized because she has seen numerous strange dogs outside the home setting. But all of these meetings are long distance or your puppy is always on-leash. You may be in for a shock when you see how your dog acts when she is allowed to be up close or off-leash around other dogs and puppies.

It can often be counter productive and even detrimental to the socialization process when one dog is kept on-leash and not allowed to interact with a group of dogs that are playing off-leash. Many dogs will pull and strain on the leash in an attempt to either avoid or engage the off-leash dogs. The dog's natural behavior is restricted, thereby resulting in the dog being forced to act unnaturally. A dog who may indeed want to play can easily appear aggressive. The dog lunges, growls, barks and strains at the end of the leash. The owner misinterprets this frustration as aggression and begins to limit the dog's encounters with other dogs. The more the dog is isolated, the more frustrated the dog becomes. When it does finally see another dog, its apparent aggressive behavior only reinforces in the owner's mind that their dog is anti-social. So the dog is even further isolated and the problem gets worse and worse.

If the pup that is on-leash is fearful, the restraint caused by the leash may make him feel unable to safely retreat. The pup often feels the need to resort to fear growling or snapping at the other dogs to make them go away. It usually works. This only reinforces and perpetuates the dog's behavior. Many dogs act anti-socially only when on-leash or restrained.

Merely seeing other dogs does not constitute socialization. In order to be socialized, your puppy needs to be able to interact freely with other socialized dogs and puppies.

Many of you provide your puppy with the opportunity to play with other dogs but then you defeat the purpose by not allowing your puppy to learn. Instead of letting the pups interact, you constantly interfere, protecting, forcing, disrupting and interrupting the learning process. Your puppy needs to make mistakes, she needs to bite too hard so she can learn not to bite too hard. She needs to jump on the wrong dog and get scolded. She needs to learn to control those big clumsy feet. Your pup needs to roll and tumble. She needs all of these experiences to develop and learn. Your puppy needs to be able to act like a puppy. You've seen your puppy tear around your house, crashing into walls and chairs. The puppy is not going to break while she is tumbling around with another puppy. Don't worry if your puppy is chased or hounded by the other pups. Don't worry if your pup yips or makes another puppy yip. Don't worry if an older dog scolds your pup for what seems to be no apparent reason. A lot is happening that you are totally unaware of because you are not a dog. All these things would happen whether you were there or not. Before humans entered the scene, who would intervene to come to the pup's rescue? Dogs lived in packs and got along just fine long before we came along to goof them up.

If you cannot stop yourself from interfering because you are truly afraid, or there is a potential problem that worries you, then find a different location or a different group of dogs and puppies for your puppy to socialize with.

In every one of my puppy classes there is always at least one puppy that is hounded, harassed, chased and sometimes even mounted by one of the other puppies. The fearful puppy often screams hysterically, runs away frantically or cowers in a corner, snapping at anything that approaches. Owners get upset, ineffectively chastising the "bully" and coming to the rescue of the "victim." When owners do not interfere, within 20 to 30 minutes the situation will have resolved itself. The fearful pup will learn that if she doesn't run, there is no chase. If she gets pounced on, it is not such a terrible thing. In fact, she learns quite quickly that this is really fun. Now the puppy is relaxed and playing. These owners are happy and grateful that their puppy has learned to play and not be afraid. They can now begin to reap all the other benefits of having a socialized dog.

At the same time, the rambunctious puppy has learned to tone down her overly friendly play with shyer dogs. She learns that if she comes on too strong, she will not have a playmate. If she behaves this way around an older dog, she will usually be reprimanded by that dog.

However, when owners cannot overcome their own over-protectiveness and continually interfere, the puppy never learns anything. The shy puppy never comes out of her shell. Instead, she becomes overly fearful and dependent on the owner. This puppy never learns to play. As such, the owner and the dog never enjoy the benefits of socialization. This puppy continues to bite the owners, treating them as littermates. This puppy destroys the house and yard looking for a way to vent her energy. Puppies that leave class in this state of fear are still unsocialized years later. Many of them call me at least once a year with another problem that is caused by the dog's lack of socialization during puppyhood.

With inappropriate interference by the owner, the overly excited puppy never learns any self-control. As an adult dog, she will always be overly rambunctious and uncontrollable around other dogs. These dogs often learn the hard way. They end up playfully jumping the wrong dog and get severely reprimanded - i.e., bitten by that dog. Puppies that are denied the opportunity to learn to play nicely with other dogs usually spend their lives restrained by the owner when other dogs are present. The excuse the owner gives is that their dog is overly friendly. What they mean is that their dog is a bull-dozer and uneducated in the realm of proper canine social etiquette.

Small Dogs

If you have a small dog that you have no intention of letting off-leash to romp with the big dogs at the beach or park, you may think it unnecessary to socialize him with other dogs. Wrong! These types of dogs are usually most at risk of serious injury or trauma. I've seen countless small dogs see another dog and go into such a frenzy of aggressive display that it provokes the larger dog to also act aggressively. As long as you can physically hold and protect your dog, he will be safe. Let's hope the larger dog doesn't end up jumping on you to get to your little beast.

In many such occurrences, the little dog gets so worked up that he leaps uncontrollably out of the owner's arms and finds himself face-to-face with a larger dog who may think he has been challenged. Now the little dog is in big trouble. A common occurrence is for the little dog to bolt in fear, possibly running into harm's way. Even if you don't lose physical control, it's annoying and embarrassing holding onto a barking, hysterical dog. You will not be able to go any place where other dogs are present without causing a scene.

The other possibility is that the smaller dog doesn't act aggressively, but he trembles and cowers in fear. This doesn't pose such a huge problem, but again, why have to avoid all other dogs just so your little dog doesn't become a nervous wreck? It's unfair to your dog to have to go through life in constant fear of other dogs. Even if your dog isn't going to run and play with other dogs, at least it would be nice to have him sit pleasantly on your lap without having a panic attack or barking obnoxiously.

Owners often inadvertently create problems by rewarding fearful behavior. They pick the dog up, talk to him sweetly and try to soothe him by saying such things as, "It's okay, it's okay." The message the dog is getting is that it's okay to be hysterical. If the dog is on leash on the ground and the owner sees another dog coming, they frantically snatch their little dog up in their arms, hugging him tightly. They usually turn away preventing their dog from seeing the other dog or they talk scoldingly to the other dog to get away. Their own emotions and behavior send a tremendous message to their own dog that something is terribly wrong. They actually teach their dog to be afraid of other dogs and that they are indeed something to fear and avoid.

It is common sense and well-advised to pick up your little dog when a larger, unknown dog approaches. But you can avoid problem behavior and attitudes on your own dog's part by doing this nonchalantly and unemotionally. Just be matter of fact about it. Pick the dog up just the way you would pick him up if you were at home and wanted to lift him up for any other reason. By simply not acting overly emotional and over-protective, you will not give your dog the wrong message. During your puppy's critical socialization period, expose him to dogs you know that are sweet, gentle and friendly with other dogs. If your puppy has good experiences with other dogs while he is a puppy, he will not grow up to be afraid of them. Now you can sit with your dog in your lap at the veterinarian's office or take your dog to the groomer and know your dog will be a relaxed, happy camper when he sees other dogs. Socialize your puppy with other dogs and you can go through life without contributing to the reputation that little dogs are yappy, snappy, obnoxious brats.

Socializing the Fearful Dog

If your dog is already past the critical socialization period and is fearful of other dogs, you may not be able to change his mind. However, you can teach him to be quiet and settle down in the presence of other dogs. He can learn this response regardless of whether he likes other dogs or not. If your dog is a trembling, nervous wreck, don't feed into this behavior. Try to find another small dog or two to begin socializing your dog. Better late than never, although the longer you delay, the more difficult it will be.

The process of socializing a dog that is shy or fearful towards other dogs is best left to other dogs. The length of time required for socialization depends very much on the dog's age. With a puppy, it may be accomplished within months or less. With adult dogs, it is much more time consuming and may take as long as a year or more.

The first step towards socializing a fearful dog is to find another dog that the shy dog likes or is at least not too terrified of, and get them together on a frequent and regular basis. After a number of meetings, the dogs will establish a special relationship.

Try to find a dog that is friendly and playful. Exposing the shy or fearful dog to a young puppy usually does the trick. A shy dog is usually not overly afraid of a young puppy. The two develop a fun relationship and in just a few months, the puppy is the size of an adult dog, so now the shy dog has at least one adult sized canine friend. This does a lot to build confidence. Then try to find another pup or perhaps a gentle adult dog as an additional playmate.

Generally, it is best for the first meeting to take place on neutral territory. Arrange to meet the owner of the other dog for a long walk in an isolated area. Walk both dogs on leash. First, do not allow them to investigate each other. At the end of the walk, invite the owner and dog over to your house. The next time, the post-walk activities may take place at the other owner's house. The longer the dogs are left together, the greater opportunity the shy dog will have to build up confidence and to begin to interact and play. Again, be careful not to reinforce shy or fearful behavior. If the dog wants to hide, that's fine. He will eventually come out of hiding. A ploy that often helps is to make a point of playing with the other dog.

Repeat this procedure with a couple of other dogs to further build up a canine circle of friends. Once the shy dog is confident interacting with each friend individually, it is time to invite two of them over at the same time. Usually the two other dogs play and the shy dog is the outsider until he gradually learns to join in.

Now it is time for more communal walks in areas where you are likely to meet several other dogs. With the presence of his buddy or buddies (both human and canine), the shy dog will have more confidence in meeting unfamiliar dogs.

Training can be a great help when socializing a shy dog. Simply instructing your dog to heel, sit and lie down each time he encounters another dog, will help take his mind off the stress of meeting the other dog. The shy dog will feel more secure since he does not have to worry about how to act. He only has to follow your instructions. In addition, instructing your dog to sit or lie down eases the tension during a canine encounter. A dog that is sitting or lying down is perceived as relaxed and non-threatening.

Consequently, the other dog will be less likely to threaten. In turn, the shy dog will feel less threatened, so the meeting is more likely to go well. This simple procedure helps to diffuse potentially stressful situations.

The two most important rules are: do not do too much too quickly; and do not unintentionally reinforce the dog's shy behaviors. Ignore any signs of fearfulness that the dog may show. If the dog becomes threatening or defensive and growls or snaps, either reprimand him with a loud "NO!" or just ignore it and leave him to back up his own threats. Never reinforce the dog's threatening or defensive behavior by reassuring or picking him up in any attempt to calm him down. If the dogs are given enough time and are allowed to meet on several fun occasions, they will usually make friends. If you are truly afraid that one dog will hurt the other, stop the play session and find a more suitable playmate for your dog.

Mounting Behavior

It is normal for dogs to mount each other. It's also normal for owners to be horrified when their virginous canine is apparently sexually assaulted by another dog. It is normal for dogs of either sex to mount dogs of either sex. Many owners are shocked and confused when their female dog mounts a male dog or another female. By constantly protecting your dog from the normal realm of dog behavior, your dog never learns how to deal with this. Instead, your dog becomes helpless and abnormally dependent on you. In the wild, who is there to protect all the dogs from each other? They learn how to deal with life, and act like a dog. Without interference from you, your dog will learn how to escape, ward off or defend herself from this unwanted behavior, if she doesn't want it. If you let her learn to handle this herself, she will have much better success at controlling the male dog than you or the male dog's owner. When you rush to save and protect her, yelling, kicking at and pulling the male dog off, she will indeed think this is a terrible occurrence and will come to rely on you to always rescue her. Instead of being confident, in control and able to handle this herself, she will become helpless every time she thinks another dog is approaching with similar intent.

Of course, please use some common sense. If an 85 pound dog is trying to mount your 10 pound dog, then it is advisable for you to interfere. I have, however, seen hundreds of socially skilled dogs of less than 10 pounds successfully ward off the advances of dogs over 100 pounds.

This is not a license for owners of male dogs to let their dogs run amok and constantly annoy other dogs by mounting them. Be a considerate dog owner - both to other people and their dogs and to your own dog. If your dog is sexually obsessed, mounting everything in sight, do him a favor and neuter him. It's not fair to let him have the equipment and then deny him use of it. How long are you going to continue to let you own ego frustrate your dog? Get over it. See your shrink. Get your dog neutered.

If you see your neutered male or female dog mounting another dog, then instead of waiting for the owner of the other dog to cause a scene, just tell your own dog to stop it. If your dog is well trained, it's an easy thing to do. If your dog is not well trained, then go over and put your dog on leash. Take your dog home and start calling some dog training schools.

When socializing your dog with other dogs, never assume all dogs or most dogs to be friendly. Never trust a dog you don't know. Allowing your dog to approach a dog you do not know to be friendly or social can result in tragedy.

Unfortunately, there are dogs that are dog aggressive, have bitten and inflicted severe injury to another dog. This dog will bite again. If you own such a dog, muzzle it whenever it might come into contact with another dog.

The best place to start socialization is in a class where you can get feedback from an experienced and knowledgeable trainer on your dog's behavior in a group of dogs.

Help! My Dog Has An Attitude!

FIGHTING

Chapter 4

As humans, we do not always have success controlling our emotions or avoiding unpleasant situations. But because our parents and society have had the good sense to socialize us, we've learned limits. A normal, well-socialized human can get angry without pulling out a knife and stabbing someone.

Just as our socialization process has taught us self-control, a well-socialized dog can get angry, scold another dog and even fight with other dogs without inflicting physical harm. Sure, there will always be the little nicks, cuts and small gashes on the muzzle, ears and legs, but this is normal. It happens in play as well as in fights. There is no need to become hysterical or fall apart over it. If we treated our children as we do our dogs, they would be in the emergency room for every scratch, cut, bump and bruise. It's abnormal for dogs to fight each other and inflict a life-threatening injury. The exception are under-socialized dogs and dogs that are bred and trained to fight.

By not socializing our dogs as puppies, we deny them the opportunity to learn normal canine etiquette and their own social language and rules. As a result, the unsocialized dog ends up constantly getting into trouble with other dogs because they don't know how to behave properly. The under-socialized dog is not prepared to meet the social demands placed upon him. When the asocial dog meets another dog he will act antisocial. He will either try to retreat or he will try to convince the other dog to retreat by acting aggressively. An insufficiently socialized dog will often walk right up to another dog who doesn't want to be approached. The under-socialized dog gets bitten in the face because she never learned how to read the dog language that says, "stay away." When an unsocialized dog bites, he usually causes severe wounds because he never learned bite inhibition. If you want your dog to get along in the canine world, it must be socialized as a puppy.

In a pack of dogs who are living without human intervention, new members are always entering the pack, i.e., puppies are born. These pups enter an established working social system which serves as the model for them. These puppies are taught the rules of the pack and social order by other members of the pack. No human is there to prevent a rambunctious puppy from being rolled, pinned or growled at by an older member. The puppies learn to respect their elders and the more dominant members of the group. The puppies learn to read the subtle body language of the adult dogs. They learn to recognize an invitation to play verses a warning that says to stay out of the way. As soon as they learn and accept the rules, they are able to behave appropriately and avoid unpleasant incidents, usually until they reach adolescence.

Adolescence or puberty is a normal developmental cycle in dogs just as in humans. Adolescent behavior usually begins at about five months of age and lasts until the dog is around three years old. During this time it is normal for the young dog to push, test and compete for a higher ranking position in the pack. (It's also normal for them to challenge the authority of their human pack. Refer to the chapters on Rebellious Biting and Who's in Charge.) Their confidence is also boosted as they begin to exert their authority over the new, younger puppies that have been born into the system.

Puberty is particularly protracted in male dogs. At about five months of age, the male puppy begins to secrete the male sex hormone testosterone. At about ten months of age, the puppy's blood levels of testosterone peaks and is almost five times higher than that of an adult dog. This hormone changes the odor of male dogs, especially their urine. It is almost as if the pup had a neon sign flashing over him advertising the fact that he is an adolescent. This olfactory sign warns adult members of the pack that the pup is maturing into an adult male dog which will soon be a potential competitor. There is an urgency at this time for the older dogs to again instruct the youth on the subject of canine social etiquette. Adult dogs, especially males, will begin to constantly harass the male puppies. The adult will stand over, growl and rest his chin on the puppy's withers. The male pup will freeze, whimper, lower his head, roll over and even submissively urinate; or challenge and get reprimanded by the adult dog.

Physical dominance plays a minor role in the establishment of social relationships. Such relationships are determined more by psychological domination. To prevent psychological harassment, the adolescent dog learns to demonstrate and advertise his respect to the adults at critical times and to maintain a low profile. Then peace is maintained in the pack not by the dominant dogs bullying the others, but by the subordinate dogs expressing their submission.

A popular myth is that fights are caused by higher ranking dogs, the so-called top dog or alpha dog. People erroneously think that the top dog is a pushy, mean bully who goes around growling and picking fights. Nothing could be further from the truth. It is the insecure, uncertain, confused dog that does this. A well-socialized high ranking dog can accomplish with a single stare or body placement what many under-socialized, insecure dogs can not convey with lengthy, noisy, threatening displays and frequent fights. The true top-dog is relaxed and confident. There is no need for noisy, threatening displays or fights. The true top dog gives a simple, subtle warning. If the warning is ignored or deliberately snubbed, then the rebuke is short, sharp and to the point. The top dog is generally not the instigator. Usually it is the lower ranking or asocial dog that threatens, attacks first or does not defer to the higher ranking dog. Many unsocialized dogs have never had the opportunity to learn this subtle canine language; therefore they respond the wrong way and get nailed by higher ranking dogs. These unsocialized dogs are either constantly getting nailed or they begin to attack other dogs as a preemptive strike before the other dog can attack them.

Fighting is most likely to occur when two adolescents (especially males) try to determine their relative rank to each other. Usually there is an lengthy bluff and threat display as both dogs are still testing each other. The confrontation may erupt into a protracted, noisy fight. It sounds as if the dogs are killing each other. However, the bites are usually inhibited as neither dog is really self confident enough to commit himself to an all-out attack. The fight is more a psychological battle than a physical one. In a stable group of dogs, these adolescents soon learn not to fight because it draws the attention of the higher ranking dogs who will come over and police the fight. If they are fighting over a commodity such as a bone, they will soon learn that neither gets the commodity because while they are busy fighting, another dog in the pack will come and take it away.

Since you, the owner, should be the ultimate top-dog in the eyes of your dog, you should easily be able to deter your dog from fighting. If this is not the case, then you need to change your relationship with your dog and enroll in a training class as well.

There are two separate issues when it comes to fighting. It is important to understand the difference between the following circumstances because different rules apply. In the home environment, fighting between dogs that live together is handled differently from fighting on public property between dogs that don't know each other. However, the rule in either case is: no fighting allowed.

Fighting Within the Pack

Although fighting is a normal canine behavior, it is actually quite rare between dogs in the wild. Fighting is very limited in a well-established group of dogs. Dogs are pack animals and have an instinctive need to fit into the pack. They have an instinctive need to know where they stand relative to each other. They don't necessarily have a need to control or rule the pack, but they are insecure if they don't know where they stand in the pack. If left to themselves with no human intervention, as dogs in the wild, they would work out their social pecking order by themselves. It is the stress and insecurity of not knowing one's standing that causes fights among dogs. In the home setting, most fights are caused by the owner interfering with the social order. Either the dogs are treated so inconsistently that they are never sure of where they stand, or the owner keeps sabotaging the existing social structure. If and when the dogs do fight, the owner perpetuates and exacerbates the problem by scolding and rewarding the wrong dog - further muddying up the waters of the hierarchy. When dogs know exactly where they stand and there are no challenges to the order, then no fighting occurs.

Bringing Home a Puppy

Most of us do all the wrong things when bringing home a second dog, especially a young puppy. In an attempt to make the new puppy feel welcome and because we feel the puppy is helpless and innocent, we unintentionally interfere with their normal social interaction. Certainly, we wouldn't have a child and then let the child dictate family policy. This is silly, of course, we are the adults; we are the responsible members of the family and we make the rules. We teach our children to be social, well-adjusted members not only of the family, but of humanity. An older dog will usually have the same instinct towards the young puppy you bring home. If you deny your more mature, resident dog the opportunity to teach the puppy the canine rules in canine fashion, you will create canine social unrest which results in constant harassment of the pup by the older dog and eventual fighting as the puppy matures. Your older dog will be constantly frustrated because she cannot do what nature tells her to do and the young puppy will run amok thinking he is the center of the universe. When this puppy encounters other members of his own species, he will have nothing but trouble because he has not learned socially acceptable and normal canine behavior.

If the resident dog is well-socialized, then she will know how to teach the new puppy the rules without harming him. Even though the older dog may growl, snap, bare her teeth, roll, pin or harass the puppy, this is normal canine behavior. Sometimes, while the two are playing, the older dog may suddenly get angry and scold the puppy in canine language. This behavior frightens, angers and confuses us because we are not dogs and we forget that dogs communicate differently than humans. As a result we interfere; we separate, we reprimand, scold and punish the older dog for doing her responsible duty. This creates enormous problems.

Turn this around in human terms for a moment. What do you think would happen, and how would you feel if you were not allowed to give your child guidance? What if you were punished every time you went contrary to your child's whims, wants and demands? Your child would probably eat nothing but cake and ice cream. Your child would never go to school and would watch TV all day. There comes a time when you as the adult must make your child eat nutritiously and go to school whether they want to or not. If you were not allowed to dictate the rules, you would be frustrated as a parent and human being and the child would end up sociopathic. It is normal for you the mature adult to make some judgement calls and rules for the child. It is normal for the mature dog to establish the rules for the puppy. It is how these rules are expressed that upset us so much. We can't expect the older dog to put the puppy on restriction, deny his allowance or just sit down and talk things out. Dogs are dogs and when they reprimand, scold or warn, they bark, growl and act like a dog. If you find this intolerably offensive or unnerving, don't get a second dog.

Dogs have a pecking order and the more dominant members have more privileges. That doesn't make them tyrants or bullies, just as it doesn't automatically make you a bully just because you have certain privileges over your children. In the dog world, rank has its privileges. The dominant dog doesn't maintain his position by constantly beating down the subordinates. The role is maintained through privilege and signs of respect and subordination from the lower ranking dogs.

You can maintain peace in your pack by not scolding or punishing the dominant dog. You don't need to scold or punish the puppy either. You need to let the dogs establish their relative order by themselves. They speak fluent canine and can accomplish the task easily and rapidly. Many owners report that they never did anything or never observed their dogs working out their ranking. This is often the case because it happens so quickly we don't see it or we don't recognize what has occurred. On many occasions the "working it out" happens when we are not home or present to observe it.

Your job is to reinforce the social order, not sabotage it. Treat the dominant dog like she is the dominant dog. She gets special rights and privileges that the other dog doesn't get. By feeding into the social structure, you maintain the order. If you start treating the lower ranking dog as if he were the top dog, then you are interfering with the set structure and undoubtedly fighting will occur.

Occasionally, a new puppy may try to dominate your resident dog, especially if the puppy is very confident and the older dog is more submissive. Sometimes the resident dog is just extremely tolerant and will let the puppy be pushy. It is best to let the two of them work it out on their own. If you don't have the heart to see your older dog get trampled by the pup, then perhaps you have chosen the wrong puppy to integrate into your home.

Bringing Home an Adult Dog

When bringing an adolescent or adult dog (generally six months and older) into a home with another adult dog present, it is best to have the dogs meet and adapt to each other on neutral territory. Neutral territory is an area where the dogs expect to meet and see other dogs. If the resident dog is suddenly and abruptly exposed to another dog right on the threshold of his own private domain, the unexpectedness of it can precipitate a fight.

Fighting is most likely to occur between dogs of the same age, sex and social rank. If you are looking for a second dog, it is advisable to get one that is different in age and sex and therefore most likely to also be different in social standing.

Case History

A married couple had a wonderful dog and decided to get another as a companion for him since they were away at work so much. They were planning a vacation soon and would be able to spend time with both of the dogs. They had to take possession of the new dog about a week before their vacation began. During this week, everything was fine. The dogs got along beautifully. This was because the owners were never home long enough to interfere. But as soon as their vacation started, problems began. Trying to make the new dog feel more welcome, she was showered with affection and attention and the resident dog was basically ignored. As soon as the resident dog showed any dominant behavior towards the new dog (lip curling, growling) the owners immediately and severely punished him. The new dog was then pampered and fussed over. Since the two dogs had already established and accepted their relative positions, the actions of the owners were undermining the order. From the dog's view, the dominant dog was being treated second class, and the subordinate dog was receiving all the benefits and privileges as if she were the dominant dog. This frustrated the dominant dog and made the new dog insecure and frightened. The new dog did not want to be treated as the top dog. In just a few days she went from a spirited, fun-loving, happy-go-lucky dog to a bundle of shivering nerves. The new dog did not even want to enter the house and if the owners forced the dog inside, she immediately found the first hiding place and cowered there until the owners let her back outside. As soon as the new dog was let outside, the resident dog immediately stood over her, growling and snarling until the owners would separate them and punish the resident dog. The owners were about to take their new dog to a shelter for unwanted pets when they called me for advice.

The Cure

The answer was simple. Let both dogs in the house. Treat the resident dog like a king. Give him special snacks in front of the other dog. Praise and dote over him for just breathing. Ignore the new dog for a while. Don't fuss over her or give treats in front of the resident dog. Feed the resident dog first and the new dog second. In other words, treat them according to the social order they had previously established and accepted. If the resident dog finds any reason to dominate the new dog by growling or standing over her, just ignore them. If the owners couldn't bear to watch them act like dogs, then they should leave the room.

In two days, everything was wonderful again. The two dogs played together happily. The new dog was once again a relaxed, happy, fun-loving dog. The resident dog had no need to dominate the new dog because the owner was now supporting rather than undermining his position. To maintain harmony, the owners simply continued to treat the dogs in a manner consistent with the established social order.

"Working it Out" Without Fighting

If the two dogs being introduced are normally socialized dogs, then your best policy should be to let them work things out for themselves. Allowing them to work it out does not mean allowing them to fight. Just as the higher ranking dog in a pack polices the fighting between middle ranking members of the pack, you too should insist on a no-fight policy as the top-dog of your own pack. Allowing them to work out and maintain their relative positions means not interfering with their own ways of dealing with it. Don't try to be the equalizer and keep everything fair and equal. Your interference here will only increase the need and likelihood of fighting. Giving special rights and privileges to the upper ranking dog will maintain peace and prevent fights as long as you remain consistent.

There are many ways that a dog can develop, maintain and exercise the privileges of rank without resorting to fighting. Following are some typical ways that the more dominant dog will exert his rank. He will pick up a toy or treat and parade past the other dog. He will drop the object right in front of the other dog without the slightest intention of allowing the other dog to touch it. Any attempt or interest in the object by the other dog will be met with an ice-cold, blood chilling stare or growl and showing of teeth. The higher ranking dog will lie across doorways or dog doors preventing passage by the lower ranking dog. The top dog will hoard all the toys and steal treats given to the lower ranking dog. It is unnatural for dogs to be treated equally. Although we might find it objectionable, dogs do not feel the need to share. Don't think about interfering in these situations, forcing them to share or making sure they are treated equally. If you do, you will probably precipitate a fight.

The upper ranking dog will sometimes not allow the other dog access to her own food bowl or the water dish. In this situation you should interfere or you may end up with one fat dog and one skinny dog! Separate their food bowls and allow them adequate distance from each other. Supervise the feeding and tell the higher ranking dog "No!" if he trys to push her away. Over time, the lower ranking dog should gain enough confidence to guard her own food.

If a Fight Occurs

If a fight does occur, immediately reprimand both dogs, then further exert your control by making both dogs do a short down-stay. Release them and allow them to interact as soon as possible. Do not take sides or give preferential treatment to either dog. Make it clear to both dogs that you will not tolerate fighting. If they were fighting over a commodity like a toy or bone, then remove it and let neither dog have it. Your policy should be, if you're going to fight over it, then no one can have it.

Your voice alone, sternly commanding both dogs to "Off," "Stop it," or something similar should be enough to stop your dogs' fighting. If your voice alone cannot stop them, this indicates lack of respect for you on the part of the dogs. You should work on gaining that respect, as well as control through obedience training.

If during a fight, the dogs inflict excessively damaging wounds, that should be a clear sign that they are not socialized enough to know their limits. If they bite without inhibition, they should be separated permanently to avoid severe injuries.

In most cases, dogs left to themselves will work out their relative social rank. If the owners have been isolating the dogs from each other and undermining the dogs' relative rank, fighting will continue because there is no resolution. The longer the owner has been interfering, the longer and more violent the fights become. A snowball effect results. Each time the dogs are separated, their level of anxiety and frustration increases. This increased tension creates more aggressive behavior. The next fight is worst than the last and the owner separates the dogs for even longer periods of time. The longer the dogs are separated, the more tension builds, the more likely the dogs are to fight when together. Each fight usually results in more injury until one or both of the dogs end up at the veterinary emergency room. At this point, it is usually too late and the dogs can never be trusted to be alone together again.

If there is a huge discrepancy in sizes of the dogs then it is probably best not to leave the introduction to the dogs. One accidental move can break the delicate legs of the tiny dog. However, a sturdy or rugged small adult dog and an eight week old puppy of a medium sized breed would probably be fine and they usually do well together even as the puppy grows and matures. This is because the smaller dog will usually teach this clumsy oaf of a pup to be keenly aware of appropriate bodily contact. The small adult dog will also learn early on to keep out of the way. There are thousands of owners who have large and small dogs living together and no problems. If you are worried about a potential problem, it's best to choose a dog that would be a more appropriate size.

Pack Dynamics

Bringing another dog into the pack can often change the behavior of the resident dog. Most commonly, a good-natured, playful dog (when it was the only dog in the house) suddenly becomes more dominant or aggressive around other dogs, especially in the presence of the new dog. Some owners like to interpret this as the resident dog "protecting" the new dog; "showing off" for the new dog; or exhibiting "jealousy." Most likely, the resident dog is simply more aware of social hierarchy or more confident now that she has another dog at home over which she can exert herself. Whatever the reason, just be aware that this sudden change in behavior is not unusual.

If you have two or more dogs, it is common that each dog individually gets along with other dogs, but when they are together, they may try to bully or "gang up" on another dog.

Fighting Outside the Pack

In a stable pack, dogs do not fight because they know their social standing, their place in the pecking order. However, in the domestic world, when a dog encounters a dog outside of his own pack, neither dog knows where they stand relative to each other. They may test each other with growling, staring and other body language. A fight may ensue.

Owners often unintentionally train their dog to act aggressively towards other dogs. When the dog growls, lunges or threatens another dog, they try to calm and soothe him. The dog interprets this reaction to mean that the owner is pleased with his behavior. In a feeble attempt to avoid embarrassment, other owners drag their dog away, sometimes even yelling or scolding the dog. This action tells the dog that something is definitely wrong and that there is good reason to be aggressive. The owner's anxiety, apprehension and retreat feeds into their dog's aggressive behavior.

Once the dog acts antisocially, it's common that we further restrict his social environment by limiting his interaction with other dogs. A vicious cycle develops: the more the social environment is restricted, the more asocial the dog becomes and behaves, hence the more his social interactions are restricted. Eventually such dogs are kept confined because they always act aggressive around other dogs.

Secure, confident, relaxed, socialized dogs don't give a hoot about whether another dog is more dominant and therefore are not inclined to start an argument over who is more dominant. These dogs are so secure in their place in the world that they have no need to prove themselves. Dogs who are insecure in their social status are usually the troublemakers. They pick fights with other insecure dogs. Since both are insecure, they both feel they need to fight to see who wins so they can determine their status.

If two dogs are normally socialized, they can probably fight and not cause any harm to each other. Once the fight is over, they will probably not fight again because they have determined their relative standing to each other. Unlike some humans who feel they can only be happy if they are Number One, dogs are not so concerned with whether they are number one, two or three. The important issue to them is that they know exactly where they do stand. However, just because the dogs can fight and not harm each other does not mean you should allow them to fight.

It should be intuitively obvious that if your dog is unsocialized or if he doesn't have an inhibited bite, then you should never let your dog near enough to other dogs for a fight to be a possibility. Dogs that have bitten and injured another dog will bite again, usually inflicting a more severe injury. If one dog has an unfair advantage due to size, health, age, etc., they may not intentionally try to hurt the other, but injury may result because of the disparity.

Most dog fights I see are fairly normal. However, I almost always then see two humans yelling at each other about whose dog is to blame. Whose fault is it? It's both dogs' fault. It takes two to fight. All one dog has to do is show a sign of submission and the other dog will have won, resulting in no need to fight.

Here's a typical case I see again and again. Rover will shoot a challenging look at Spot. If Rover is unsocialized, he might not realize that his look was a challenge. Spot accepts the challenge and lunges over at Rover. A fight results and Rover's owner claims that for no reason at all Spot attacked his dog. It's really Rover who started it. But Spot could have just ignored the challenge. So both are at fault. Unfortunately in this case, Spot is usually punished and "poor, innocent Rover" is pampered and cooed over, making him feel he was right to challenge and fight. However, because the fight was broken up before it was settled and Rover was then rewarded for fighting, he will probably continue his challenges to other dogs. The next time these dogs see each other, they will most likely fight again.

In this scenario, the owner's usual comment is, "Spot likes most dogs, but for some reason he just hates Rover." Another observing owner might say, "All the dogs at the park get along fine. Only I can't understand why so many dogs seem to pick on Rover."

Solution to Fighting

Once past the socialization phase of development, the primary solution to occasional fighting on the part of your dog is obedience training. Your dog should trust and respect you enough that all it takes is one command from you and your dog becomes unconcerned with the other dog. If your dog is secure enough with you as the owner, and is well trained, then your dog will listen to you. If your dog has no respect for you, then your dog is going to do whatever he wants to do and you will have no control over him. If this is the case, finish reading this book and immediately seek the help of a professional trainer. It's never too late to obedience train your dog.

If your dog is involved in a fight, you need to reprimand him immediately. Make it absolutely clear that you vehemently disapprove of this type of behavior. Then whatever good time the dog was enjoying before the fight should be terminated. If you were out on a walk, march right home. If the dog was romping in the park, put him on-leash and take him home.

If you let your dog know that you disapprove of fighting, he will avoid fighting other dogs out of respect for you. He may still want to fight, but he will control himself because of your presence. However, it's important to realize that if you are not there to control him, most likely he will engage in fighting if the opportunity presents itself. You can train your dog not to fight with other dogs but you cannot train him to play with other dogs. Play with dogs will be the dog's decision. You can encourage play by rewarding and praising your dog if and when he does engage in playful behavior.

Some dogs are actually taught to fight or act as if they dislike other dogs. Every time their owner sees another dog, their body language, voice and actions tell the dog that something is wrong. By becoming terrified yourself or by pulling your dog back and away from other dogs, you may be signaling to your dog that these other dogs are indeed something to dislike, to be afraid of or even protect you from. Other dogs act wildly, leaping, barking and lunging at the end of the leash. Because the owner allows this to go on, the dog has no idea that this is inappropriate behavior. I've seen many cases like this cured instantly when the owner finally had enough moxie to simply tell their own dog to knock it off. By spending time with your own dog and by watching dogs interact, you will be able to determine when you should avoid a situation or not. Instead of waiting until there is a dog fight, you should just prevent it by watching your dog whenever he is off-leash. At most dog parks I go to, the owner lets their dog off-leash and then sits down to read a book or begins talking with other dog owners. Because they aren't watching their dog, they don't see the fights coming. If they simply monitor their dog, they could easily see a potential problem and avoid it. All they have to do is call their dog to come, or give him a command such as "off" or "leave it." If you don't have off-leash verbal control of your dog, you have no business letting your dog off-leash to begin with. It would be the same thing as giving your car and car keys to a nine year old.

If you have a dog that missed out completely on socialization and is an aggressive dog that likes to fight, then you have only one option. Don't let this dog near any other dogs without the help and guidance of a professional trainer. Be responsible and muzzle him for the public's safety.

Once a dog has severely bitten or attacked another dog, you should assume that he will absolutely do it again if given the opportunity. Even with extensive training, no dog is 100% predictable. You must realize that if you lose control for even one second, the result could be devastating.

Castration

Neutering a male dog greatly decreases the incidence of fighting with other male dogs. It is most effective when done very early, before the dog reaches adolescence. Neutering after adolescence usually does not make the dog less aggressive. However, there are indirect effects on social interactions that can reduce the frequency of fights. The castrated dog may still be aggressive, but he will not be perceived as a male dog by other dogs. As such, other male dogs will not consider him as much a threat, so they stop challenging him. Since other male dogs will act less aggressive, the neutered dog will feel more relaxed and less likely to issue challenges himself. No challenge - no fight.

Separating Fighting Dogs

If your dog is involved in a fight and your voice alone cannot stop him, you need to interfere and stop the fighting as soon as possible. Be careful so you are not bitten yourself.

Here's a few effective methods to try. It's best not to touch the dogs with your hands if you can help it but if you must, grab each dog by the tail, rump or back legs and pull them apart. Don't reach for the face and head area (where the teeth are). Be careful. Many dogs will turn around and bite whatever or whoever is grabbing for them - even their owners! Throw or spray water at full force in their faces. Throw a jacket, towel or blanket over the face and head of either one or both of the dogs and pull them apart. Continuously poke or jab the bristle end of a broom or some similar object at the dogs' mouth and face until they stop fighting or are biting the broom instead of each other.

Help! My Dog Has An Attitude!

PLAY BITING
RECKLESS BITING

Chapter 5

Some of the most painful bites I've ever experienced have been play bites. An excited dog leaps up to grab a tennis ball while playing fetch. The dog gets the ball all right, but she also clamps down on my hand at the same time. The bite wasn't intentional; the dog didn't mean any harm; it was an accident; but it is still a bite.

While playing tug-of-war, the dog haphazardly grabs at the toy, misses and bites your hand. While jogging, your happy, excited dog nips at your pant legs. Eventually the teeth connect with skin and results in a bite. You come home from work, your exuberant dog is leaping about wildly to greet you. She jumps up at your face in usual style, but this time she nips at your chin or ear, resulting in a bite. You offer the dog a treat and he ravenously snatches the food right out of your hand, chomping down on a finger.

However you may rationalize, when dog teeth injure human flesh it is called a bite. The reason is incidental. One of the worst excitement bites I have seen was from an exuberant miniature breed dog leaping around on the owner's lap. The dog's teeth caught the owner's ear, ripping it open resulting in a slice that required many stitches.

Never allow your dog to bite you in play. If you let your dog bite you in play, what you consider gentle and painless may be painful and cause bruising on a child or elderly person. If the dog becomes excited, the gentle biting quickly gets out of control and becomes hard and painful biting.

The very fact that the bites occur in play, in greeting or as an accident causes us to excuse and ignore it. We feel guilty and think it's unfair to scold or reprimand our dog while she is playing, having fun or when she is just happy to see us. The dog soon learns that she can act haphazardly and recklessly around us. We have taught the dog that there is no need to exercise caution or to be respectful. We have taught the dog that it is okay to be out of control. We have taught the dog that biting is acceptable. Not only will the dog think it is all right to bite us, but she will also think that it is okay to be careless and disrespectful.

This is not what dogs do to each other. They don't rationalize and make excuses. Biting and disrespect are so swiftly and effectively reprimanded that it rarely, if ever, happens again. If you observe an established group of dogs interact and play, they don't make mistakes with each other. Higher ranking dogs do not tolerate disrespect from puppies.

A three month old puppy is developmentally similar to a five year old child. You would probably think it fairly disrespectful if a five year old child suddenly jumped on you and started pounding, kicking, pulling and jabbing, even if just in play. You would not be too pleased to be used as a punching bag, springboard, or walking plank. There are times to play, but the adult is not ambushed. Children and parents make agreements as to when, where and how to play. Parents also make decisions as to what is appropriate play. You wouldn't consider it agreeable for your children to play with a knife and furthermore poke you with it. This is not acceptable play. A dog's teeth are its weapons and should not be used on you in play. Dogs are hunters and predators. Their teeth are designed to be able to kill to eat.

If a child gets out of control and becomes overly rambunctious, we have no qualms about telling the youngster to settle down. But we literally and figuratively allow our dog to walk all over us. Do not be afraid of hurting your dog's feelings. You should teach her to be careful and respectful, especially with her mouth.

Dogs are not humans; we cannot reason and have discussions with them. It does no good to try to communicate with them in "human." You must communicate in "dog" language if you want them to understand. They learn from the consequences of their actions.

Watch how the mother dog or higher ranking dog reprimands a puppy or subordinate dog. It is a quick, volcanic, vocal eruption right in the dog's face. The dog is not harmed. It is a momentary, psychological explosion. Never hit, slap, spank or kick your dog. An effective reprimand is immediate, verbal and directed right in the dog's face. The reprimand should be instantaneous and swift enough to catch the dog by surprise.

It's extremely easy to teach the rules to a new puppy. A few repetitions will probably do the job. If however, you let the biting go on and on, it is increasingly more difficult to stop. It is also dangerous to yell at a dog who already thinks she can boss you around and get her own way. She could actually turn on you and reprimand you for daring to reprimand her. The dog may bite you again but this time not in play. Therefore, it is important to set the play rules very early. Start as soon as your new dog arrives home.

Be sure your rules are consistent or your dog will never be able to figure them out. If you let the dog get away with biting 30% of the time, she will continue to bite. If at any time you let the dog get away with biting, then she will learn that biting is okay some of the time and so she will continue to bite. You must adhere to an absolute no-bite policy. Do not allow one single bite to go unreprimanded.

Some owners wait until they receive a serious bite that requires emergency care and stitches before they effectively reprimand their dog for biting. In other words, they wait until they are genuinely angry. Don't wait. You have to be a little theatrical and pretend that you are angry long before the bites become that bad. Most owners are emotionally unable to express anger at their dog until it is too late. Instead of stopping the biting behavior early on, they wait until it has become an ingrained habit. At this point, it becomes increasingly more difficult to stop the behavior.

Other owners tell me that they do reprimand their dog but when I observe them, they act and sound like a giant squeaky toy. Their demeanor is fun and play rather than scolding. If your scolding only seems to get your dog more excited, then obviously your reprimand is not being taken seriously. Change your tone or attitude. Your dog can see right through you and if you don't really mean it, your dog will know you are just kidding and therefore, will continue to bite.

Dogs, especially puppies, need to play and to be able to act like dogs. Again, here is where socialization with other dogs is so valuable. You should play with your dog, but not as a littermate. You need to find other dogs and puppies for your dog to play with. She will learn valuable lessons about how hard she can bite and how roughly she can play. She will learn to be gentle with more fragile dogs and she will learn to be respectful of more dominant dogs. It is desirable for your dog to bite in play, but only with other dogs, perhaps the family cat, if the cat approves, and of course with toys.

Following is a simple exercise to practice with your dog regularly as a constant check on his biting and as a reminder should he make a mistake.

When your dog is in a spunky, energetic mood, get out a super yummy treat. Use something that you normally would not give him, such as cheese, a bit of pizza or a potato chip. Wave the treat around to get him interested and excited and then offer it to him by holding it between your thumb and index finger. If he is respectful, he will take the treat without biting your fingers. Praise him profusely and give him several more treats in like manner. However, if he gets careless and bites your fingers, then instantaneously reprimand him by screaming bloody murder right in his face and do not let go of the treat. Offer it again. Only let him take the treat if he does so gently, and tell him, "Good dog."

Most dogs will immediately tone down their exuberance once they have been reprimanded. Never let your dog recklessly snap food or toys or anything from your hands. If you feel that your dog may just bite you in the face if you try this exercise, then do not do this. Go to thechapter on "Who's in Charge" and start there.

Tug-of-War, Rough Housing and Mouthing

Traditional advice warns that it is a bad idea to play tug-of-war games with your dog because it can make the dog aggressive. I have found that most owners ignore the advice and do it anyway. The reasons are simple: we enjoy it too much; the dog enjoys it too much. If played properly, tug-of-war and rough housing games are some of the best anti-aggression exercises you can practice with your dog.

Tug-of-war is a wonderful game because it is fun and it does provide a way for you to play with and exercise your dog. However, it can lead to problems if you do not abide by certain rules when playing. If you ignore these rules, then you shouldn't play. If you abide by the rules, then you can and should continue playing.

Rule #1.

While playing tug-of-war, most dogs will make a mistake and grab at fingers or hand instead of the toy. While rough housing, the dog will mouth the owner. Because we are playing a game and feel that the mouth or bite was accidental or just in play, we ignore it. Big Mistake! This teaches the dog that it is okay to mouth or bite us.

Everyone who allows their dog to mouth or bite in play eventually complains later on that the dog bites too hard. What you consider a gentle bite may be considered painful by someone else. If one member of the family allows the dog to mouth or bite in play, the dog will be uncontrollable by other family members. It's entirely too confusing for the dog to learn that it is acceptable to mouth some people and not others. The dog will also be confused about what is play and what is not play. Dogs that are allowed to mouth or bite in play will also mouth and bite when being handled or groomed. The dog may think you are playing when you're trying to remove a foxtail or burr from her paw. Every time you put your hands on the dog, she will think it's rough house and mouthing time.

Even if the dog does not bite hard at the moment, it will become extremely annoying. If the dog realizes that you are not playing, she will continue mouthing, trying to turn an unpleasant situation into one of fun and play. Dogs will also use this play biting as a way to sneak in complaint biting.

Those owners who allow their dog to bite in play are unable to distinguish between play biting and complaint biting. In the long run, they always complain about the biting getting out of control and regret that they ever allowed it in the first place. Once you allow your dog to mouth or bite you in play, it's extremely difficult to break the habit. But it can be done.

If you allow rough housing or tug-of-war, you must never allow the dog to mouth or bite for any reason. The instant the dog's tooth or teeth touch you or your clothing, you must immediately reprimand the dog and stop playing. Scream "Ouch!!" right in your dog's face, snatch the toy away and do not play again for at least one hour. Let your dog know that you absolutely will not put up with her being reckless and careless with her teeth. If your reprimand is performed correctly, your dog will become acutely aware of what she does with her teeth, especially when she is excited.

To make the dog even more keenly careful about tooth contact, you should try to trick the dog into making a mistake. Suddenly change hand positions after you've invited the dog to take the toy. It seems unfair to set the dog up to make a mistake, but by doing so you will be fine-tuning the dog's agility and awareness. It is really not such a difficult thing for the dog to do and learn. A dog can move her mouth infinitely more quickly than you can move your hand. This may amaze you, but then you are a human, not a dog. Dogs may be amazed that we can open cans of food. It's not a big deal to us, we have an opposing thumb, dogs do not. There's no mystery here. It's basic physiology.

Dogs by nature are tuned into body position and movement. A dog would never accidentally touch a higher ranking dog with her teeth. If you let your dog step all over you and bite you, then the dog is learning she doesn't really need to respect you. If you let your dog mouth or bite, you should not play these types of games.

Rule #2.

The dog should never be allowed to initiate the play session or grab for the toy without invitation. The dog is allowed to take hold of the toy only when you tell her she can by giving a command such as, "take it." If you allow the dog to initiate or grab without invitation, then you will suddenly be playing tug-of-war with your socks while you are trying to put them on. When you go out to pick up the morning newspaper, you don't want the dog to suddenly grab the other end and start tugging. Even if the dog is playing, it will be considered obnoxious, dangerous and aggressive for your dog to suddenly run up to a person and start tugging on their belongings.

If your dog brings her toy and prances around or drops it at your feet, then the dog is requesting a game. This is acceptable if you want to play. If so, then ask your dog to say, "please," by giving her a command such as sit-stay or by heeling the dog around the living room once before engaging in play. If you do not feel like playing at the moment, then tell your dog to bug off or settle down or some other command you've previously taught her meaning to leave you alone and not be a pest.

Rule #3

Whenever rough housing or playing tug-of-war, you must stop the game every 30 seconds. In addition to stopping the game, insert a five to ten second training session between rounds of tugging. After 30 seconds of play and tugging, simply stand still, look your dog in the eyes and tell her to, "Drop," or "Give," or some such command. As soon as she lets go of the toy, praise profusely, ask her to sit, down, stand stay, then give the "take it," command and resume the play session. This is a constant reminder to the dog that you are in charge and in control. It rewards the dog for instant compliance. It also prevents the dog from getting out of control.

If the dog does not respond to the "Give" command, immediately take the toy away and stop the game because you have just proven that you are not in control. If you cannot control the dog or she does not know how to "give" or to sit, down, or stay, then you best not play these games until you train your dog to do so.

Help! My Dog Has An Attitude!

REBELLIOUS AND COMPLAINT BITING

Chapter 6

The average dog owner today needs to point a finger at themselves and take a good hard look at how they may be abusing their own pet. Most people assuage their guilt by pointing their fingers at what the press and animal rights organizations expose. Cruelty to animals is a horrible thing. The average owner can be just as guilty of it, only our methods of abuse are much more subtle, insidious and generally unrecognized, overlooked or condoned.

There are over two million dog bites reported each year. An even greater number of bites are unreported. Most dogs that bite people are euthanized. People have little tolerance for an aggressive dog. First we inadvertently train our dog to be aggressive, then we kill him for being aggressive. A little unfair, don't you think? It is extremely abusive for owners to not provide instruction to their dog, then later on spank, scold, get rid of or euthanize the dog for behavior that the dog never even knew was wrong.

Our emotions prevent us from being objective and fair. It's easy to over-indulge and spoil a new dog or puppy not realizing that this could very possibly be abuse in the long run. It doesn't seem like we are doing anything wrong, but every time we give in to our dog's whims, we are planting the seeds that can result in violent, aggressive behavior later on.

When we pick the puppy up and he struggles, we immediately put him down because he obviously doesn't want to be picked up right now. If we try to hold and look at his paws and he struggles or pulls away, we immediately let go. If the dog doesn't like it, we think we shouldn't do it. Through accommodation, we teach the dog that he doesn't have to do anything he doesn't want to do. All he needs to do is resist, struggle, whine, growl or complain and he will get his way. Then the day comes when we must make the dog do something against his will. For instance, putting him in the car to go to the vet. The dog doesn't want to go in the car. He bites when we try to force him. The dog's toenails are getting too long, causing him to limp. The dog doesn't want to have his feet touched, much less his nails clipped. He must be muzzled so he doesn't bite the groomer. The dog has an ear infection, but he won't let you medicate him. The dog is asleep on your bed; you need to move him over so you can get in bed too, but the dog doesn't want to budge or be moved or bothered. So you end up sleeping on the couch because you don't want to get bitten. These things happen with alarming frequency.

Eventually your dog will have to do something against his will. If the dog is used to getting his way, he will protest when he doesn't get his way. If you insist on pursuing your course of action, the dog will feel forced to bite you (or the vet or groomer or. . .) in an attempt to get you to stop. You suddenly realize that you have a problem. What you don't realize is that you created this problem way back when you first brought the adorable dog or puppy home.

It's normal for dogs to test and see what they can get away with. It's our responsibility to train them to be civil. From the first day you bring your new dog home, let him test you, but instead of teaching him that he can get his way by thrashing, struggling, whining, growling or biting, show your dog that you will get your way. If your dog gives in, which he will if you have more patience than he has feistiness, then the dog will learn that it is exceedingly more rewarding to give in and comply with your wishes than it is to struggle trying to get his own way.

The following exercises are extremely easy to do with a young puppy and most small to medium-sized dogs. If you feel that you cannot do them because of your dog's size, strength or temperament, then don't do them. If your dog resists out of fear or lack of trust, refer to those chapters that deal with that issue. If your dog is aggressively rebellious, postpone these exercises and refer to the section on "Who's in Charge." Once you've gained your dog's trust and respect, you can return to these exercises.

Exercise #1

Lie the puppy down on the floor flat on his side. There is nothing uncomfortable, unpleasant, complex, difficult or threatening about this position. In fact, all dogs on their own will lie on their side while resting or sleeping. But as soon as you try to make them do it, they may object simply because you imposed it on them. Don't let the puppy up no matter how long he struggles or carries on. Do not scold or get angry. Just wait it out. This is now a battle of wills and you must show your puppy that you will win. He must do what you want him to do whether he wants to or not. You will not make unreasonable demands on him but when you do want him to do something, you should expect that he will comply and not bite you or struggle in protest.

This particular exercise is performed by dogs on dogs as well. If you ever get the chance to observe a litter of puppies with the mother dog or observe a stable, established group of dogs, you will see the more dominant members of the pack, literally pin and hold down a subordinate but rambunctious or disrespectful puppy. Some dogs will sit on the subordinate, others will lie down on them, but the result is the same, the higher ranking dog holds or pins the puppy until he stops struggling. But you are going to add something to the exercise.

As soon as your puppy stops resisting and struggling, praise him immediately. Stroke his tummy, massage his back. Do something you know your puppy finds pleasant and rewarding. Hold your puppy there a little longer, praising and petting all the time he is calm. Reward your pup with a super delicious treat. In no time at all, the puppy will learn it is much more advantageous to relax and comply than to struggle. Struggling is useless anyway because he never gets his way. Make sure your puppy continues to lie still and relax after you have eased your hold on him. Some pups will relax while you are holding them down but as soon as you relax your hold, they will immediately spring up and bolt away. This is equivalent to them getting in the last word. Don't let this happen. Be ready to grab the dog immediately and require him to continue lying still even after you have relaxed your hold. If you start this exercise the day you bring your new puppy home, it will probably take only a couple of days and a few repetitions to have a completely relaxed, compliant pup. It may take longer with an older puppy.

Exercise #2

Once your puppy is showing no signs of resistance to lying on his side, gently roll him over on his back for a tummy rub, or as if you were trying to teach him to roll-over. He should allow you to do this without resistance, complaint struggling, whining or biting. Proceed as in the above exercise.

Exercise #3.

Begin with your puppy lying relaxed on his side. Gently touch and inspect your dog's entire body. Get him used to having his ears looked into, his mouth opened, his feet touched and nails clipped. Touch and handle your puppy the same way a veterinarian or groomer would. Then proceed with "child-proofing" your puppy. Get him used to being touched and handled in slightly obnoxious ways. Do not hurt your pup but do a few annoying things that a child might do. Tug his tail, pinch his rump, grab and squeeze - gently mind you, these are not meant to hurt, just annoy.

During these exercises, most pups will mouth and bite in protest or in play. If your puppy tries to do this, you must immediately reprimand him with a short, sharp verbal outburst right in his face. At the same time, continue holding the puppy down on his side. After the pup has relaxed, start praising then immediately test to see if your reprimand got through. If holding his paw caused the bite, then take hold of the same paw again. If the puppy learned his lesson, he will not bite you this time. However, if your reprimand was ineffective, the puppy will bite you again as soon as you hold his paw. It's his way of saying, "Hey, I thought I told you not to touch my feet. Stop it right now!" Repeat your reprimand but try to be more convincing this time. Repeat the test and reprimand until the pup stops biting, then reward and praise the pup.

Each and every time your puppy allows you to touch and handle him without struggling or biting, lavish him with rewards and praise. With this method, your puppy will learn not just to tolerate these things, but to actually enjoy them.

Many owners are reluctant to do these exercises for many reasons. They are either afraid of the dog, or they don't want to hurt the dog's feelings, or they think it unfair to set the dog up to bite just to reprimand him for biting. They don't see that they are actually setting the dog up to succeed so he can learn not to bite. In any case, consider this: When your dog mouths or bites you in protest to being handled and you do not stop it, then you are creating a time bomb. Mouthing is your dog's polite way of telling you he doesn't like what you are doing. If you don't stop annoying your dog, he will eventually get angry and really bear down on you resulting in a bad bite.

If your dog complains about being handled, you have a few options:

1) You can simply avoid handling the dog or doing anything he dislikes. This way he will be in total control. The dog will call the shots because he will know that if he doesn't want you to do something, all he has to do is complain by mouthing, growling or biting.

2) You can continue to handle the dog and ignore or tolerate his complaints. If you do this, you are taking the chance that one day he will tire of complaining and will decide to severely bite you or a person trying to touch him (a child, the groomer, the veterinarian . . .). If he bites the wrong person, the law will take the dog away and have him destroyed.

3) You can teach your dog to accept and enjoy being handled and that protesting, mouthing and biting are not acceptable behaviors.

The choice is yours.

Once you feel that your dog is compliant, respectful and happy to be so, that doesn't mean your job is over. The rest of your interactions with the dog must be consistent with the roles you have established. Your daily routines should always include these exercises, which will become fun and rewarding for both of you.

Here's a heart warming story about one of my students. At least, this is the type of thing that warms my heart. Chibi is an adorable 12 pound dog. His owners are a very quiet, gentle family. He came into class huddled in a blanket, nestled in the owner's arms.

When I approached to say hello, he growled and snapped at me. The owners all held up their hands and showed me an assortment of wraps and bandages around their arms and fingers. He cowered in fear at all the other dogs and looked suspicious of all the other owners. I could tell how much they loved this dog but I guess they finally decided they had to do something about the biting. Their veterinarian sent them to me because she thought it ridiculous having to muzzle a 12 pound dog for a routine vaccination.

I immediately ascertained that the dog was spoiled. They concurred. At home, he ruled the roost. He gave them hours of joy and affection but if he didn't want to do something, he simply rebelled by biting. Needless to say, he was also the worst dog when it came to the obedience exercises. He simply refused to do anything and the owners felt helpless as well as afraid of their own dog.

All we did was change the owners' attitude. Instead of protecting and indulging him, they just ignored his fearful behaviors. The most difficult thing to get them to do was raise their voice at this little dog. As soon as they were able to raise their voice at him, they found a new confidence in themselves. Chibi also noticed their new confidence. The owners were tired of having the worst dog in class. They were embarrassed that this miniscule beast was controlling them. All it took was a few good verbal reprimands for biting, as well as not spoiling him at home to change his entire demeanor. He still got everything he wanted at home, but not unless he performed the obedience exercises that were being taught in class. Suddenly, he was willing to obey. Previously, he knew he didn't have to do anything because he would get his way anyway.

In 6 weeks, Chibi was a new dog. Everyone in class applauded not only him but the family as well. They saw this dog change from being fearful, aggressive, rebellious and disobedient to being a happy, friendly, trained dog. At the last week of class, Chibi was climbing in my lap and kissing my face. He even played with the other dogs instead of cowering away from them. The owners were bandage free. He had the best down-stay of all the dogs in class.

TRUST AND CONFIDENCE

Chapter 7

The quickest way to teach your dog that you are not trustworthy is to punish your dog with physical violence or to reprimand him for some action that he is not presently engaged in.

Punishment is never appropriate for dogs because by definition it is a consequence for some past action. Let's draw an analogy so you understand how punishment is perceived by a dog. Suppose you are sitting at your desk at work and your boss barges in yelling at you in a foreign language as he drags you out of your chair. You'd be confused, anxious and wonder what in the heck is going on! You may cower or get angry and defend yourself against the onslaught. When a dog is punished, he feels the same way. The dog may cower: ears back, head down, tail tucked, "please don't hurt me." In this case people erroneously stand in judgement, "See! He knows he's been bad," thinking the dog actually knows what he's being punished for and furthermore feels guilty about it. Alternatively, the dog may feel the need to ward off the violence by growling or biting. Now the dog is labeled aggressive and untrustworthy when all he was trying to do was defend himself.

Physical violence such a hitting, kicking, slapping or spanking your dog will only result in the dog anticipating abuse when similar movements toward the dog begin. The dog may be too fearful to bite you, but someday the dog will bite someone else. Let's look at the owner who spanks his dog with a newspaper. The dog doesn't have the confidence to defend herself against the owner so she just takes it. One day a guest is over and picks up a newspaper. The dog sees this and thinks she is going to be hit again. But the dog is not afraid of the guest, so she defensively attacks and bites him to prevent what she thinks is going to be another violent encounter. The entire incident seems unprovoked. Because the guest was so overwhelmed at the attack, he forgot he even picked up the newspaper. Or he remembers but it seems irrelevant. All that's remembered is that he was walking across the room when suddenly out of nowhere the dog leapt out and bit him. This kind of bite is very common. Because the attack is apparently without provocation, these dogs are labeled unpredictably aggressive and are usually euthanized. Unfortunately for the dog, these are not unpredictable or unprovoked bites. The cause of the bite is the owner. Anytime you strike your dog you are eroding the dog's trust and setting the stage for a future aggressive incident.

The Dog's Confidence

It's natural for dogs to regard certain things we do to them as unpleasant. It's not much different than how we humans feel about going to the dentist. The experience is usually unpleasant but we tolerate it because we know it's for our own good. We may not like what the dentist does, but we don't leap out of the chair and attack him or her. Many dogs attack their care-givers including their owners. Countless owners are bitten by their own dog when simply trying to inspect an ear or paw.

With a little foresight on your part, your dog can learn to tolerate this type of handling with ease. Long before you find a foxtail in the dog's ear, get the dog used to having her ears touched, looked into and cleaned. If done properly, your dog will look forward to ear inspections because it is the prelude to something terrific, such as a game of fetch, a run at the park, a nice long walk, a relaxing massage or a yummy treat. By associating an unpleasant activity with something the dog really loves, you can teach your dog to accept and even enjoy the activity. If you do not particularly like having your teeth cleaned but were given $1000 cash everytime you did, you'd be making trips to the dentist weekly, if not daily. You can develop the same happy anticipation in your dog by rewarding with the doggy equivalent of $1000. It's a simple task to build the confidence of a very young puppy. Their minds are uncontaminated and unprejudiced. But with an older dog, the process of confidence building can be an extremely lengthy process.

Here is an example of the process involved with a dog that did not receive proper confidence building exercises as a puppy. Brandy is one of my rescue dogs. She was about 2 years old when I took her into my pack. At the mere sight of nail clippers, she would hide and shiver under the bed. Any attempt to reach for her made her growl defensively. I was sure if I pushed the issue, she would bite me. However, Brandy must be part retriever because the sight of a tennis ball turned her into a beaming, happy puppy-like dog. So for several months I paired the clippers with the tennis ball. I would hold up the clippers in my left hand and then immediately produce the favorite tennis ball with my right hand. At first she didn't know whether to run away or stay for a game. If she ran away, nothing happened. I just ignored her. If she stayed we played a long and vigorous game of fetch. We also did not play fetch at any other time. It wasn't long before the mere sight of the clippers made her jump in delight knowing it meant she was going to play fetch. This response is not unlike the dog who leaps about wildly when the owner gets out the leash. Or the cat who comes running when it hears the electric can opener. The leash signals a walk. The sound of the can opener heralds dinner time. In Brandy's case, the clippers signaled game time. Once the sight of the clippers did not bring on a fear response, but instead a happy response, we were ready for the next step. Now the routine was: clippers appeared, but before playing fetch, I would momentarily touch one of Brandy's paws. At first she seemed suspicious but when we immediately began playing fetch, she forgot all about it. Again it took several months of this routine before she showed no signs of apprehension at having her foot touched when I was holding the clippers.

Over the months, the fleeting touch on her foot turned to longer touches, short holds and finally extended massages. When she would happily tolerate having her paw held and massaged for the reward of the game of fetch, I proceeded to touch one of her nails with the clipper. No cutting yet, just touching clipper to nail. Then we proceeded from touching the nail to a quick snip off the tip of just one nail. It took several days to clip one nail. Finally it was one nail a day. Over one year later, I could produce the clippers and Brandy would roll over on her back and allow me to clip all 18 nails in one sitting. I always paid off with a nice long game of fetch. Today she will settle for a small treat, a quick massage or big hug and kiss of approval.

How I wished that whoever had her as a puppy would have done these exercises with her then. The entire process would have taken a week instead of a year. Don't let this happen to your dog. If it's too late for your dog, then you can certainly try the desensitization process but it requires an enormous amount of patience on your part. Get your dog used to being touched and handled, picked up, hugged, restrained, bathed, groomed, etc. Don't forget child-proofing exercises. Teach your dog to accept annoying handling such as what a child may do or what you might inadvertently do. I've been bitten several times while just trying to stop someone's dog from running into the street. I would see a dog bolt away from its owner and head straight for a busy street. In an attempt to "save the dog" I had no choice but to abruptly grab onto it wherever I could as it zipped by. One dog I was able to grab by the collar, another dog I grabbed by the tail, yet another I grabbed by the fur on his back. I successfully stopped each of these dogs from running in front of a car, but they all bit me. So be sure to get your dog used to being reached for, grabbed, pinched, squeezed, tugged and pulled at. These are things that dogs might find annoying and it would be tragic for an overly friendly child who is just trying to say hello to your dog to get bitten in the face. Teach your dog that there is no reason to be afraid of anything physical that you do to it. Teach your dog to relax and enjoy these activities.

Your Confidence

Some of you have dogs that refuse to be touched or handled not because they lacked confidence but because you lack confidence. I see people who are actually afraid of their own little puppy. I can understand being afraid of your full grown 95 pound dog, but if you are afraid of your 9 pound puppy, you have no business owning a dog. If you are afraid of your own puppy, then you will not do the confidence building exercises and therefore your puppy will never learn to accept or enjoy being touched or handled. Your pup might have easily learned to trust you but your own fear prevented it. However, if you do the exercises properly, both of you can become confident with each other. Why have a dog that you cannot touch? Why have a dog that you have to avoid when she is eating, sleeping or "in a bad mood?" I often see dogs come to class totally ungroomed. The fur is matted, the ears are filthy, the nails are too long. And it's not because the owner doesn't love their dog, it's because the owners are afraid of their own dog. If they try to brush the dog, she growls at them. If they try to touch her feet, the dog bites them. If you are not confident and do not trust your own dog, you will never be able to teach your dog to be confident and to trust you.

POSSESSIONS

Chapter 8

I't's very easy to unintentionally train your dog to be aggressive and protective about food, bones, toys or just about anything else. Many of you have probably already done this but won't realize it until one day your dog bites you or someone else. Here are the ways in which we have already screwed up. (Unintentionally, of course!)

First, anytime we feed our dog his food or give him a bone, we usually simply hand it over and walk away. Sometimes we feed the dog in some out-of-the-way area or corner of the house, yard or garage. We don't want to disturb the dog and possibly upset his stomach with any activity occurring while he is eating. We tell everyone else to leave the dog alone too. Anytime the dog is eating or chewing on something that he is allowed to have, or something that we have given him, we leave him alone. All these things cause the dog to get used to dining in privacy. Any approach later on may be regarded as an intrusion or threat. In an attempt to maintain his privacy, the dog may act aggressively.

However, anytime the dog has something we don't think he should have, we act quite differently. If the dog has a sock, a shoe, a twig or a paper towel, we suddenly turn very possessive and immediately take these things away. At the start we easily succeed at taking these forbidden items away. But what we are doing is setting a precedent. Whenever the owner approaches the dog while he is chewing or eating something, chances are extremely high that the item will be taken away and the dog will never see it again. If no one approaches, the dog retains the item and can chew or eat in peace.

Then one day the dog finds a chicken bone in the park. You go to take it away and the dog thinks, "I've got you figured out; if you take this away I'll never see it again." Consequently the dog will feel he needs to protect his "find" by warning you to stay away. He growls. If you do not heed the warning, the dog may snap or bite you. If this happens, you are so shocked that you don't know what to do, so you do nothing. Now you have successfully taught the dog that by growling or snapping, he can control you and keep the object. From then on, anytime the dog has something he doesn't want you to take away, he will growl or snap to protect it.

Keep Away

Instead of growling, other dogs will quickly take the item and run away knowing that you can't catch him. You get sucked into a game of keep-away. The dog has learned that by avoiding you, he can keep the object. He knows that if you catch him, you will take the object away. Some of you, frustrated and angered by the chase also physically punish the dog if you do catch him, giving him even more reason to avoid you. Even if your dog is good natured and you don't punish him, he will continue to deliberately steal items just so you will chase him. It's a fun game and he loves it. You might even play into the game, actively teaching your dog that this is the behavior you want! You may not mind until he steals something that matters to you.

Soon, anytime you look at the dog when he has something, or take one step towards him, he will take the item and run. The dog may not bite you but you certainly have a problem. If you catch the dog, he will clamp down on the object and not give it up. If the item is dangerous, it spells bad news.

Some dogs will resort to other means of keeping objects or not giving them up. If possible, the dog will quickly swallow the item before you have a chance to take it away. I've seen dogs look like vacuum cleaners. It appears as though the dog instantly inhales the item. I've seen entire socks, plastic baggies, rubber toys and plastic bones go down-the-hatch in less than a second. Now we're talking life-threatening behavior, needless and expensive veterinary care and surgery. These dogs continue swallowing and eating the inedible even when you are not trying to take the object away. It has become a self-rewarding and self-perpetuating habit. As soon as the dog sees a baggie, he runs over to it and scarfs it up. The dog has learned to be fast and sneaky and at this stage it is extremely difficult to change the dog's attitude and behavior.

Instead of backing off when the dog growls, some owners excessively reprimand the dog without ever building its trust and confidence in them. Severe reprimands and punishment around items or food can actually make the dog more protective and aggressive. When the owner approaches the dog while he is eating something, the dog will growl not only as a means of trying to protect the object, but also as self defense against the owner's violent behavior. If the dog is too afraid of the owner, he may not bite the owner, but sooner or later someone else will be bitten.

Few owners are bitten more than once by their own dogs around food because the owner knows better and simply avoids bothering the dog when he is eating. However, many outsiders are bitten. They didn't know the dog was protective. Many of these bite victims were not trying to take the item away from the dog. All they did was inadvertently get too close, causing the dog to think he was being threatened. The dog leaps out and bites as a means of preventing the person from getting any closer. Common example: a person drops a pencil and bends down to retrieve it. The dog is nearby chewing a bone and thinks the person is bending down trying to reach for the bone. The person is bitten.

Most owners do not take possessiveness seriously. They erroneously assume it will simply go away. They make excuses for the dog. Most of them say it's natural for a dog to be possessive. And they're right, but that doesn't make it acceptable. Unfortunately, they won't realize this until it is too late. It isn't intimidating or frightening when a ten pound puppy snarls so it doesn't occur to them that they might have a problem. Every dog that I've seen exhibit aggressive behavior as a puppy continues to be aggressive as an adult dog unless the problem is dealt with immediately and swiftly.

Some owners want to wait to see if it really becomes a problem later on before they do anything about it. Don't wait until you or someone else is bitten before you admit that you have a problem. Don't wait until you have to rush your dog to the veterinarian for emergency surgery because the dog has swallowed a bottlecap that you couldn't take away from him.

If your dog is already aggressive with possessions, the first step in curing the problem is to regain control, respect and trust from your dog. See the appropriate sections, especially, "Who's in Charge?" Then commence with the food handling exercises described here. Begin with a Mikki style muzzle (one that allows eating and drinking) on the dog until you feel confident that the dog will not bite you. When working with objects, be sure they can not be swallowed whole by the dog. Do not work for extended periods of time. Always end on a success. Since the muzzle inhibits panting, don't work on warm days. Don't forget that stress also makes a dog pant. The idea is that you've worked long and hard enough on reclaiming trust and respect from your dog that there should be no tension performing these exercises.

The good news is that possessiveness is extremely easy to prevent. The following exercises can be performed easily and effectively with young puppies and dogs that do not already exhibit possessive aggression.

Be Patient

When you first bring your young puppy home, begin immediately to win his trust and respect. Don't set a precedent of letting him eat or chew in privacy. Don't set a precedent of always taking away forbidden items. Just as a human baby puts everything she touches in her mouth, so does a puppy. It's part of the natural developmental process. In the wild, there is no human present to constantly prohibit puppies from chewing on leaves, twigs and whatever he finds in his environment. If left undisturbed, the puppy will pass through this stage and distinguish between edible and inedible. Your responsibility is to provide a safe environment for the puppy just as you would a baby. Obviously, don't leave razor blades, safety pins and hundred dollar bills lying around. If the item is truly dangerous, harmful or valuable, then why was it there in the first place? You cannot create an absolute risk-free sterile environment for your puppy but you must allow him to learn, develop and mature as a normal dog. So provide lots of exciting safe items for the pup to taste, test and explore. Don't panic just because your puppy is chewing on a twig. Plants can be poisonous, so find out ahead of time which ones are toxic and get rid of them. Sometimes a puppy will eat something inedible like rocks but usually only when the owner has already interfered by constantly trying to take things away. Even if you don't make an issue of the puppy exploring with his mouth, occasionally a puppy will ingest something that will require veterinary attention. This is just a fact of life. But statistically, this is very rare. The point is, interfere to make the environment safe, but do it before the fact, not during or after.

Confidence Building

There will be times when you will have to take things away from the dog. Instead of waiting until that moment comes and not knowing what will happen or ending up in a struggling match, practice now and get your puppy accustomed to it. Taking something away from your dog should be as quick and simple as switching stations on your radio. It should be something that you or anyone else can do with confidence and ease. You shouldn't have to think twice about it. It should be equally as easy for your dog to give up an object or his food to you or anyone else. The dog shouldn't be worried, stressed or hesitant to let you take anything away. He should do so willingly, happily and immediately.

Many people are under the false assumption that if the dog has a forbidden item that the proper thing to do is to exchange items. Let's say the dog has a shoe. Some owners think it is enough to take the shoe away and substitute it with one of the dog's toys. This is only half right. Your action still shows the dog that the item taken away is never seen again. Other people have the false notion that it is also enough to exchange the item for a treat. This too still tells the dog that the item will not be returned. One of these times the dog is going to say, "No, I don't want to exchange this chicken bone for a rubber toy or even a milkbone." The two methods just described are on the right track but are missing the most vital step. The item must be returned. But no one does this because the only time they take something away from the dog is when they don't want the dog to have it in the first place, so they do not give it back to the dog. Your dog needs to know and have the confidence that the object you are taking away is not going to disappear forever.

Set the precedent and maintain it by returning the goods 99% of the time. Then the one time you do not return it because it is indeed a dangerous or valuable item, then you haven't set the wrong precedent. You haven't broken the dog's trust and confidence in you. In order to do this, you need to set the dog up and take advantage of opportunities when it will be okay to return the object to the dog. Instead most owners ignore the dog if he is chewing or eating something that is allowed and only approach the dog when they are going to take the item away. This is a bad precedent to set.

Several times a day, when you see your puppy chewing on something, simply approach the pup with a tasty treat. Most pups will immediately stop chewing their toy to see whether or not they are going to get the treat. Take the toy away, lavish the pup with tons of praise while giving him the treat and then most importantly, give the toy back. After a few days of this, you won't need to let the pup know you have a treat. Just approach, take the object away, reward verbally and then return the item. With this approach, you are rewarding the puppy for letting you take the item but you are also setting a precedent that the item will be returned.

Instead of waiting for the dog to chew on a shoe you accidentally left out, set the dog up with a wide variety of safe objects that you can practice with. Leave out a couple of socks that already have holes in them. Toss an old, worn out shoe down for you to practice on. Wad up a couple of paper towels or kleenex. Puppies usually love to shred up paper, so leave a few harmless pieces of paper around. Don't wait until the dog finds the telephone bill that you dropped on the floor. You won't want to return that, but you can certainly return a discarded envelope.

Don't be distracted by the fact that you are allowing the puppy to chew a sock, shoe or paper. These items are not to be left out all the time. If you always leave socks around, then you are also teaching the dog that socks are toys and you will be feeding into the habit of sock-chewing. These are sporadic training sessions for the two of you to practice these exercises with items that the puppy isn't accustomed to playing with. And even if you or the dog do decide that socks are indeed chew toys, then it's still far better to have a dog that chews socks than to have an aggressive, untrustworthy dog.

At mealtimes, teach your puppy some respect and restraint as well as trust in you. Don't simply put the food bowl on the floor. Ask and make the puppy sit and wait momentarily before eating. Some owners allow the puppy to jump up at the food and begin eating before the bowl even touches the floor. Show the puppy that there is no need to be frantic. The food is coming, the puppy should be patient.

Teach your puppy to accept and enjoy your approach, touch and taking away of the food bowl. Show your puppy that there is no need to be protective or defensive. Show your puppy that it is a marvelous thing when you approach him while he is eating. Most uptight, possessive dogs become very still and stiff when someone approaches. You know you have arrived at what you want in your puppy when you see him relaxed and wagging his tail in happy anticipation as you approach.

Start at a time when your puppy is not extremely hungry. Perhaps feed him 3/4 of his dinner and then half an hour later, do the exercise with the remainder of his food. While the puppy is crunching away on relatively boring, bland dry dog food, approach the pup and toss a small chunk of chicken in his bowl. After several repetitions of this, the dog will see immediately that it is extremely beneficial and rewarding whenever you approach and reach towards his bowl. Your actions are showing the puppy that you are approaching to give rather than to take. On other occasions, touch and pet the puppy as you toss the treat in the bowl. This will show the pup that there is no reason to feel threatened just because he is touched or petted while eating. In fact, you are again showing the pup that it is preferable to be approached and touched while eating. If no one approaches and touches, then he only has dry kibble. The super treats appear when the human is around. When the puppy is obviously thrilled with this exercise, then you can take the food bowl away while he is still eating, sprinkle a handful of goodies in the food, then return the bowl. This will show the puppy that it is indeed good news when you take the food bowl away because it is always returned in better condition.

If your puppy growls at you during any of these exercises, you must immediately reprimand your puppy as described earlier. Usually one effective reprimand and your puppy will never growl at you again. If the pup continues to growl or tries to snap and bite you, then stop the exercises and refer to the sections on how to earn your dog's trust, confidence and respect. If your dog doesn't trust or respect you, these exercises will be useless and probably dangerous.

Once you feel that your dog has enough confidence not to become possessive or aggressive, that doesn't mean you are done. These exercises must be perpetuated for the life of your dog. If you stop the exercises, chances are your dog might develop an attitude of protectiveness later on. It only takes a few seconds a day to maintain your dog's pleasant attitude.

FEARFUL
AGGRESSION

Chapter 9

The biggest cause of fear biting is lack of socialization. Dogs that do not like or are afraid of children are dogs that were not properly socialized with children. Dogs that fear or bite only men are dogs that were not socialized properly towards men. Dogs bite people in fear because they were not properly socialized with people as a puppy.

Some owners tried to socialize their puppy but their attitude towards the process caused it to backfire or fail. Anytime they thought a situation was too overwhelming or anytime their pup showed any signs of apprehension, they immediately became over-protective. Their attitude and behavior towards the puppy rewarded and reinforced the shy behavior. They ruined the socialization process and taught the puppy to be even more insecure and asocial.

Some owners are at the other end of the spectrum. If the puppy shows any signs of shyness or caution, they become impatient. As an over-achiever, they try to force their dog to be friendly. You cannot push, force and shove socialization down a dog's throat. This will only cause the dog to become even more hesitant.

Many people secretly want a shy and fearful dog. It feels good to have a frightened puppy run and jump into their arms for comfort and security. They want a dog that is overly dependent because it makes them feel good to be wanted and needed. There is nothing wrong with having a shy and dependent dog as long as the dog doesn't become a monster. A dog that is overly dependent gets stressed when left alone. She will often not eat when the owner is away. The dog will whine, bark and become destructive when left alone. It may make the owner feel good when their dog hides between their legs when a person approaches or passes by, but this usually doesn't last long. Most of these dogs will eventually start lunging and snarling at passers by. Eventually no one will be able to walk by, look at, talk to or pet the dog. Instead of being proud of their dog in public, these owners become embarrassed. Sooner or later, they will stop going for walks because they either cannot control their dog or because the dog becomes too upset when outside. By avoiding these unpleasant situations, the dog is further secluded and her fear and over-dependency escalates. Many owners of these kind of dogs can not have company over to the house because the dog is uncontrollable, even dangerous. Answering the door to accept a UPS package becomes a major event.

There is a very short window where socialization must occur. Some studies claim the peak socialization period is between 3 and 12 weeks, others claim between 7 and 14 weeks. In either case, most of us do not get our puppy until she is between 6 and 8 weeks old, which does not leave much time for us to delay the socialization process. If it doesn't happen within this time frame, it is so difficult and so time consuming that most people do not succeed in doing so. Even with extraordinary efforts, sometimes it is just plain impossible to socialize an older puppy or dog. If your dog is kennelled or sheltered from people for the first 4 to 6 months of her life, it would be the equivalent of keeping a human child in a closet until he or she is between 7 and 12 years old.

Unless you want a major challenge, when you buy a puppy be sure the breeder did not isolate the puppy in a kennel. A responsible breeder will not only have begun the socialization process with other dogs and people for you, but he/she will also have begun to socialize the puppy with handling, grooming, car rides, changes in the environment and so forth. Do your homework when selecting a puppy. Don't get a puppy just because you like the way she looks. Research the general characteristics of the breed. Many breeds have a natural propensity to be shy, leery of strangers and "one-person" dogs.

Most breeders will expound on their dog's good points. As far as they are concerned, their breed has no bad characteristics. This is true. Traits are not bad, they just are. Shyness or disliking of other dogs are not bad traits in and of themselves, however, they may be undesirable traits for you and your lifestyle. If these traits lead to fear biting and fighting, then you have a problem. Ask the breeder about the breed, but more importantly ask breeders of a different breed. Talk to groomers, trainers and veterinarians. Then be aware of the slant these people could possibly put on the breed.

Preventing Fearfulness

Introduce your puppy to as many people as possible - all kinds of people - large, short, tall, old, young, different sexes, ethnic backgrounds, etc. Provide the opportunity and that's about all you have to do. Let your puppy experience and enjoy at her own pace. Do not force or shove the puppy into the arms of everyone. Don't let people force themselves on your puppy either. Allow the puppy to be the one who approaches to say hello. Make sure your puppy is hungry and you have a plentiful supply of tasty treats available for the people to offer to the pup. Your hungry puppy will quickly approach a pleasant stranger offering her favorite treat in an outstretched hand. If the puppy wants affection, let her ask for it. If the puppy comes up and wants to be hugged and cuddled, fine. If not, don't force it. If your puppy is playful, allow the strangers to play with the pup. If your puppy has wonderful, fun and pleasant experiences with people, your puppy will be socialized to them. Ask several friends to come over more frequently so they can help you with the handling and confidence building exercises discussed earlier. By having people other than yourself touch and handle your pup, it will be easier for other strangers, such as the veterinarian and groomer to handle your pup.

The two biggest mistakes owners make while attempting to socialize their dog are rewarding fearful behavior and forcing the issue. Fight all your parental instincts to soothe, calm, pick up, hug and talk soothingly to your puppy if she shows signs of fear. All this does is reward the pup for her behavior. At the other end of the spectrum, control your impatience and do not get angry. Some of you want your dog to be friendly so badly that you push and force the issue, scolding the dog for hiding, shying away or retreating. This will undoubtedly make your puppy even more hesitant. Not only will she be afraid of strangers, but now the presence of strangers is paired with an unpleasant experience. This will cause the puppy to retreat even more, causing you to become even more impatient.

Growling and Fear Snapping

Many owners inadvertently but blatantly reward their dog for growling or snapping. They are often embarrassed that their dog does this or they do not take it seriously. Consequently, when the dog growls or snaps at someone, they laugh and giggle. Others give a feeble, half-hearted attempt at reprimanding the dog but their tone is so gentle that the dog interprets it as praise instead of disapproval. The dog may not be fearful at all. This may be purely a learned behavior taught by the owner. The dog thinks that the owner wants her to act nasty, and the owner mistakenly thinks the dog is afraid of or doesn't like people. Sometimes all you need to do is change your behavior and the puppy will change her behavior.

In class I see many pups growl at people and the owners actually reward the behavior. When the dog acts friendly, they ignore it. All we change is the owner's feedback. While the dog is acting friendly, they are to praise, reward and treat her. When she growls, they are to instantly yell "NO!" right in the dog's face. As soon as the dog stops growling, they immediately start praising her again. With most of these dogs, consistent and immediate feedback from the owner changed what would have been an aggressive dog into a friendly one.

Socializing the Fearful Dog

Socializing a shy dog and helping him build his confidence is a risky and time-consuming task. Using this method, it took me over two full years to socialize my two-year-old fearfully aggressive rescue dog. I succeeded, but it was a lot of work. Thrusting your dog into the arms of every visitor or dragging him outside to socialize with strangers is counterproductive and dangerous. If I did this with my rescue dog, surely someone would have been bitten. Do not endanger your friends, guests or strangers if you think your dog might bite them.

Strangers should never be allowed to approach the dog and pet him. It should always be left up to the dog to make the first contact. If the dog does not want to approach, that is OK. Give him plenty of time to "hide and peek" and eventually he will come out of hiding. Let your dog come out of his shell in his own time. Provide him with the opportunity and be there to praise, reward and encourage his new confidence. Remember not to reward his fear.

The goal is to give your dog the opportunity to meet people on his own terms. It is important therefore that participants are not allowed to approach your dog, reach out for him or do anything that might make him feel pressured or forced into meeting them. Do not do this exercise if your dog is also territorially aggressive or if there is any chance the dog will bite your guest. If in doubt, start the exercise with a muzzle on the dog. Also refer to the section on territorial aggression. Expose your dog to one person at a time and let him build confidence in several steps as described below.

1. Invite a person to your house. Before the visitor arrives, put your dog in a back room and have your guest sit quietly in a chair. Tell your guest not to speak to or even look at your dog. Then release your dog from the back room and allow him to investigate at his own speed. If he is allowed plenty of time he will learn that this person is no threat.

Do not force your dog to approach and do not pull him out from a hiding place. This will only slow things down. You can try to speed things up by offering a reward gradient around the visitor. Scatter pieces of food around the visitor with your dog's favorite treats closest to the visitor. With this set up, your dog can approach to get a treat and the closer he gets to the guest, the better the treat he gets. Each time he approaches he is rewarded and gains confidence, and the closer he approaches the more he is rewarded and the more confidence he gains. Obviously, this method will work best when your dog is hungry.

There are no fixed rules for confidence building exercises. If your dog hides in the back room, then there is no point in setting up a food gradient in the front room. Instead, the lower end of the gradient must extend to the dog's hiding place. It may take several afternoons or evenings a week with the same person before your dog feels comfortable about approaching. However, your dog may quickly decide that fear takes a back seat to a healthy appetite and he may eagerly approach the visitor in a few minutes.

2. Once your dog will readily approach, it is time to entice him to establish first contact with the guest. If your guest simply lets an arm dangle over the side of the chair, your dog might have enough courage to steal a quick sniff. Now your encouragement and praise can be helpful. Have your visitor hold some food treats and slowly toss one towards your dog, or just let them drop to the floor. If things proceed smoothly, the visitor may try holding an especially tasty treat in an outstretched hand. Once your dog will take food from your guest's hand, the guest may try holding his hand closer and closer to his own body to get your dog to approach even closer. All the while you are praising with, "Good dog, good dog," whenever your dog approaches your guest.

3. The next step is to get your dog to allow the visitor to make contact. The visitor should entice your dog to approach using a treat, then delay giving the treat for a few seconds so that your dog becomes accustomed to staying close. Next the visitor should try to reach out slowly and gently scratch your dog under the chin before giving him the treat. If the dog balks, he does not get the food. Your dog will quickly learn that in order to get the treat, he must first let himself be touched - first one scratch, then two scratches and then three scratches and so on. Within time, the first fleeting contact turns into a healthy bout of gentle scratching and stroking. Now it's time to introduce a new guest to your dog starting with step one.

Any time your dog growls or snaps you must not let that behavior go unreprimanded. However, you must be the person to scold the dog. Never let a stranger scold your fearful dog or it will only confirm the dog's fear. If the dog growls and needs to be reprimanded, then that also means that you are probably trying to force the socialization process too rapidly.

You can work on socializing your dog outside your home as well. Go for a walk with the intent of meeting various "strangers" along the way. These "strangers" are your accomplices - friends and family. If the dog growls when the stranger is three feet away but doesn't growl if the stranger is six feet away, then work at a distance of six feet for awhile. At six feet, the dog will not growl, so she can be rewarded and praised. Reserve special treats for this occasion so the dog will begin to associate the special treats with the presence of the stranger. Then close the distance to five feet. When the dog is comfortable with the stranger at five feet, then progress to four feet away and so forth. Eventually the distance will be zero and the stranger will even be able to touch the dog without her showing any fear. With a young puppy this process can be accomplished in a couple of weeks. With an adult dog, you use the same technique but the starting point for the stranger may be 20 feet away. It can takes months to years to get from 20 feet away to three feet away to finally zero.

Obedience training can also be used to get your dog's mind off a stressful situation. Instead of letting your dog act like a maniac by lunging and growling at people, train the dog to sit-stay whenever a stranger is around. This relaxes the dog and allows her to let you handle and be in charge of the situation.

This method will fail if you try to rush the dog into things. Start at a distance far enough away for you and the dog to succeed. If you constantly try and fail at too close a distance, this will only reinforce the dog's obnoxious behavior.

You must set your dog up to succeed even if you have to start at 200 feet away from the stranger. When the dog succeeds, she can be rewarded, so she can learn. The more the dog succeeds, the more she is rewarded, the quicker she learns. If there is never any success, there is never any reward and the dog never understands what is expected of her. Instead, she only gets a lot of practice at doing the wrong thing. You get angry, the dog knows it but doesn't understand why or how to rectify the situation. All she knows is that whenever a stranger is present, you get upset and so the dog gets upset too. You both feed into each other's behavior.

Help! My Dog Has An Attitude!

TERRITORIAL AGGRESSION

Chapter 10

Many of us want our dog to protect our family, our home and property. At least we want them to bark and alert us to the fact that a stranger is outside, even if our dog is not necessarily large enough to be a deterrent herself. However, if we leave it up to the dog's natural instincts, we will surely be disappointed. Unless we actually teach and train the dog how to behave, it will behave inappropriately.

If you want your dog to sound the alarm when there is an intruder, you must teach her to do so. Otherwise she might just snooze away while the burglars waltz your stereo right out of your house. In some cases, the dog is stolen along with the goods.

Some dogs are overly territorial and bark at everything. They alert the entire neighborhood when the trash collectors do the rounds. They alert the neighborhood again when a squirrel trespasses into the backyard. You and the neighbors soon learn that your dog is a habitual barker. The burglars also know that no one will pay attention to the dog when he barks because he barks all the time. In addition, the incessant barking helps mask the noise of the break-in and robbery.

You cannot leave it up to the dog to decide how and what to protect. Too many of you praise your dog for barking or growling when someone is at the door, yet later on, punish the dog for growling at the girl scouts delivering their cookies. Eventually, the dog becomes so noisy and unmanageable when someone comes to the door, that you end up locking the dog in a back bedroom or outside. What good is your deterrent-protection dog when the stranger at the door can hear that he's locked up?

Very few people end up satisfied with their dog's protective instincts. Most end up complaining that the dog is out of control. Instead of your dog being a protector, he becomes an unwanted liability. If you allow your dog to be overly protective in your home, the behavior usually transfers to other situations. Too many owners complain that they can't take their dog for a walk anymore because the dog is growling, lunging and snapping at everyone.

In the beginning, people with large, menacing-looking dogs are usually quite proud and pleased when their dog growls at a stranger. They reward the dog for acting protective. It makes them feel tough and secure - until one day they realize they can't control the dog any longer. I can't tell you how many times I have seen a person dragged across the street by their own dog that is going after a mother and child or an elderly gentleman walking a miniature dog. Now, your supposed protection dog is a mean, aggressive bully who likes to terrorize the innocent and helpless. There are just as many tragic stories of the dog biting family members, especially young children - the very people the dog was supposed to "protect."

Don't let your dog's territorial behavior become a source of danger and tragedy. If your dog is already excessively territorial, there's good news and bad news. The good news is that this problem can be cured; the bad news is that it will take a lot of time and energy on your part to retrain the dog.

First you must make sure that your dog knows you are in charge and while there is a need to alert you to the presence of a stranger, there is no need to protect you from everyone he encounters. You must have your dog's respect otherwise when you tell him how to behave, your dog will look at you as if thinking, "Who do you think you are to tell me what to do?" You must obedience train your dog so that when you tell him to down-stay and be quiet at the front door, he absolutely will do so. In the car, your dog must be able to down-stay in seconds. While on a walk, your dog must be able to heel, sit and stay regardless of distractions. If you can't control your dog when a tennis ball bounces in front of him, you certainly won't be able to control the dog when there is another dog, cat or child around.

It is not difficult to train a dog; it just requires time, patience and commitment on your part. Too many owners want their dog doing PhD level obedience in two weeks. If you want to play at Wimbleton, do you think you can do it after three easy lessons in tennis? Of course not. To develop any skill requires constant repetition and practice. Not only that, but it requires proper repetition and practice. I have people report to me that they practice walking the dog for three miles every day but the dog still pulls on leash. What they don't realize is that the only thing the dog is learning to do for three miles a day is pull the owner along. The dog becomes a stronger, better, more skilled leash-puller because that is what he is practicing. If you practice the wrong thing, you will end up being quite good at doing the wrong thing. If you do not know how to properly train your dog, then seek professional help.

Others of you complain that you can't control the dog and make him stay when someone is at the front door. I understand! One can't answer the door to accept a package from UPS and train the dog at the same time. Once the dog is trained, then all you should have to do is tell your dog, "down-stay" when you answer the door and he will. But not during the teaching phase. Until your dog is able to perform such a task, don't ask him to. If you do, the dog will fail and get yet another round of practice at failing to 'down-stay' at the door.

Alert Barking

When the doorbell rings and your dog rushes to the door barking, first say to your dog, "Alert! Good dog, Alert." Then say "enough" and start a down-stay with the dog. This will teach your dog that it is okay to alert, in fact, it is desireable, but when you want it to stop, it stops.

This is impossible to teach when you actually need to answer the door to greet guests or receive a package. You cannot train your dog and do something else simultaneously. So what do you do? Enlist the help of a friend or family member and post them outside. Have your helper ring the doorbell every 30 seconds while you work on training the dog. You don't need to answer the door, all you need to do is train your dog. By having your helper ring the bell every 30 seconds or so, it also gives you and your dog the opportunity to succeed. At the first sound of the doorbell, most dogs are entirely too excited to realize that a training session is in progress. After the 10th or 15th ring, the dog will start to settle down and be able to concentrate on the lesson.

Do this on-leash at first to make it easier for your dog and you to get started. Now all your dog needs is practice.

Apply this principle of setting the dog up in situations where you need to gain control and practice, practice, practice. If your dog barks at anyone passing by the car, then drive to a busy street, park the car and teach your dog to down-stay and be quiet. You will have loads of opportunity to practice because you are in no hurry to go anywhere. You are not trying to drive and train the dog simultaneously.

If your dog is growling, barking or lunging at people because he is not socialized, you can still train your dog how to behave with practice and repetition. However, you should also be working on socializing the dog. Go back and read the appropriate sections on this subject.

Help! My Dog Has An Attitude!

CHILDREN

Chapter 11

We all have the fantasy that our dogs and kids will be best of friends. The children will have a constant and trusting companion. The dog will teach the children the lessons of love and responsibility. The dog will protect the child and even perform Lassie-type rescues if the child is in danger. Although we read about these types of dogs and indulge ourselves in Hollywood stories, it is best to be realistic. All too often, the combination of dogs and children spells trouble, if not tragedy.

Dogs do not always adore babies and children. Dogs must be socialized with children and instructed how to behave around them. Children too must be taught how to treat dogs - with respect. Dogs are not toys and many young children do not have the capacity to understand this concept. You, as the responsible parent must provide guidance and supervision. This may seem to be common sense but when I receive hundreds of calls every year concerning dogs that bite children, I wonder.

It is far better to take preventive measures than to try to train an older dog to accept children. Bend over backwards to socialize your young puppy with children.

It's easy for dogs to be uncomfortable with the way children act, move and speak. Young children can be noisy, boisterous, and rowdy. Children do not understand that their actions can be annoying, threatening and challenging to dogs. The simplest gestures can be interpreted as teasing and provoking. When a dog feels bothered, harrassed, threatened or challenged, they don't run to Mommy or Daddy to complain. Dogs usually say "Bug off!" by growling, snapping or biting.

Begin socializing your puppy with children at three months of age or sooner. Refer to the sections on socialization and handling. Teach your dog to accept and enjoy being gently touched and handled by children. Do not let children "rough up" your dog. Children's movements can be awkward and just because your dog enjoys your touching and handling does not necessarily mean he will enjoy the same from a child.

Make sure your dog is gentle with his mouth so he can accept a treat from the child without biting the child's fingers with the treat. Having children offer the dog his favorite food treat is an easy way for the dog to realize that children are wonderful. Involve the children in controlled games that the dog enjoys, such as come here

- sit - shake hands - roll over, or fetch. Have the child instruct the dog to come, sit and stay before offering treats or throwing a ball. This shows the child that the dog is intelligent and can respond to commands. This also shows the child how to control the dog. The dog too realizes that the child is intelligent and can indeed speak in a vocabulary that the dog understands.

If your dog is already fearful of children, then don't expect that someday he will romp and cuddle with them. Instead, begin with obedience training your dog so you are confident that you can control your dog around children. Then begin the socialization process by the previously discussed methods of socializing a fearful dog. Counter-conditioning and distraction training can also be very useful when teaching your dog that children are not something to fear.

Never put yourself and your dog in a situation that can get out of control. If your dog is growling at or showing its teeth towards children, then avoid tragedy and either keep your dog away from children or muzzle him when around children.

Even dogs that love children can unintentionally harm them. A playful dog can jump up and easily topple a child. Dogs often mouth and play bite or nip at running, giggling children. Even an over exuberant wagging tail can smack a child in the face, sending him or her to the ground. No matter how trustworthy your dog is, never leave him unsupervised around young kids. Accidents happen very quickly.

It's common for dogs to be extremely friendly and playful with kids. Since children spend much of the time running and playing with the dog at the dog's level, many dogs view their human playmates as littermates. As such, the dog will be tolerant and accepting probably over 99% of the time. However, if the dog feels equal to or superior in social rank to the child, he can very easily get into a situation where he feels he has the right or need to issue a reprimand by growling or snapping.

If the dog views the child as a littermate, it will often bite the child over territory or possessions. The child tries to encroach on the dog's space while it is sleeping. The child tries to take food or toys away from the dog. The child hugs the dog, placing his or her arms over the dog's withers. This is the area where a dog trying to exert dominance over another dog will place its own chin or paws. The child tries to kiss the dog when the dog doesn't want to be touched.

Be sure your dog does not regard your children as littermates. The children must have the same respect from the dog as you do. One way to help accomplish this is to make sure the child can give commands and the dog will obey. The child must show that he or she is responsible enough to control the dog or they shouldn't be given the privilege of playing together without your close supervision. In addition, your child must be taught how to interact with the dog.

If the dog currently sleeps in bed with you and you are expecting a baby, teach your dog now to sleep on the floor near the bed. This way your dog will not be suddenly banished from the bed when the baby arrives, possibly resulting in the dog trying to regain access to the bed through territorial aggression. Instead, the dog will already understand that your bed and all beds are a "people place." This sends a strong message to the dog that the new baby should be respected as "people," not regarded as littermate. Do not be concerned about how the dog feels about sleeping on the floor.

Do not feel sorry for the dog. As long as you praise, reward and provide an occasional massage while she is lying on her rug at the side of the bed, she will be fine.

Some parents inadvertantly train the dog to be suspicious of the kids by excluding the dog from all events that involve the children, especially babies. While it is a must to separate the dog and baby at times when you cannot give them your undivided attention, the dog must be included as much as possible in routine events. Instead of putting the dog outside, or banning the dog from the nursery, train your dog to do a long down stay while you are changing diapers or feeding the baby. Give the dog a special treat at baby-feeding time. Teach your dog to heel so he can be taken for walks and strolls with the family. Ideally, this training will be done long before baby arrives, but it is never too late to obedience train a dog.

Do not let your dog regard children as a sign of bad news. In a well meaning attempt to show the dog to be respectful of a child, many owners punish the dog for acting defensive or fearful of children. While the dog does need to be reprimanded for aggressive behavior, the feedback from the owner must not be limited to reprimands. In a very short time, the dog may figure that it is the presence of children that makes the owner upset, uneasy, angry or violent. It becomes a self-fulfilling prophecy, because when the dog does growl, sure enough, the owner does become aggressive. The dog finds itself in a no-win situation. The owner creates a dog that is more and more fearful or aggressive towards children.

Instead, you need to set the dog up to succeed in being relaxed around children and reward that behavior. If the dog is relaxed, you too can relax. Then the dog won't pick up on your uneasy feelings. The dog needs over 100 rewards for proper behavior before it is ever reprimanded for improper behavior. With this method, the dog will realize that it is not the presence of children that causes the owner to get angry, but the dog's improper behavior that causes the owner to get angry. At the same time, the dog will most likely start regarding children as "good luck charms." Every time a child appears, so does the dog's favorite treat. In fact, the only time the dog gets this favorite treat is when children are present.

WHO'S IN CHARGE HERE?

Chapter 12

The Spoiled Rotten Dog

Most owners with spoiled dogs are so proud of themselves. Their face beams and their eyes twinkle when they confess that their dog is spoiled. The dog is sometimes a child-substitute and they treat their dog as if he were a helpless infant. They don't have the heart to say no. They cannot bear the thought of their dog not having his every whim fulfilled. They feel guilty every time their dog looks at them with those big, beautiful, sad eyes. They don't care that their spoiling has also resulted in growling and biting. They don't care until something unfortunate happens and animal control comes to take their dog away.

Fortunately, most spoiled dogs only bite their owners. They don't get a chance to bite anyone else because the owner protects the dog from being upset enough to bite someone else. "Oh, don't touch Junior, he's in a bad mood today." "Don't talk to Junior, he doesn't like to be disturbed while he's eating." "Don't sit there, that's Junior's favorite spot and he doesn't like to be bothered when he's sleeping."

When spoiled Junior bites the owner, they are quick to justify it. "I should have known not to touch him there." "He didn't mean any harm." "It wasn't a bad bite, I just bleed easily." "I shouldn't have tried to make him do something against his will." "It's hot today." "Fleas make him especially cranky." "I deserved it." Personally, I don't care that their own dog bites them. But I do care when their spoiled dog eventually bites someone else. I care about the bad reputation dogs have because of the example these dogs set. I care about the bad advice these owners give others concerning dogs. When tragedy does strike, I care that these owners are not able to do anything to save their dog.

By not spoiling your dog, I don't mean that you cannot give him anything and everything your heart or his heart desires. Let me tell you how my dogs live. They are allowed on the furniture. They are allowed to sleep in my bed. They eat human food right from my fork. They lick ice cream from the other side of my cone. When I eat popcorn, they eat popcorn. They have hundreds of toys. They go for walks and runs and rides in the car. We rough house and play tug-of-war. Their life may be much like your dog's life.

What's the difference? My dogs appreciate what's given; a spoiled dog takes it for granted. My dogs earn and deserve their indulgences; a spoiled dog demands it. My dogs regard these things as gifts and treats; a spoiled dog regards it as a birthright. My dogs are indulged but not spoiled. It's not what you give your dog, it's how you dispense the goods. My dogs' life is based on my terms, not their terms. We have a proper relationship. My dogs trust and respect me. I trust and respect my dogs. I treat my dogs like dogs, not infants. My dogs treat me like their leader, not a littermate.

Like most spoiled dogs, your dog is sweet, wonderful and affectionate over 99% of the time. But everything is always on his terms. If your dog is in a good mood, you can do anything. If your dog feels like it, he will even be terrifically obedient and apparently compliant. But he only acts this way if he thinks there is something in it for himself. In other words, he doesn't do something because you want him to, he does it only because he wants to do so. However, if he does not happen to want to do something, he simply will not. The spoiled dog does only what he wants to do, when he wants to do it. The spoiled dog also wants you to do what he wants. The dog is the master, you are the servant. If you do anything to cross the dog, he may growl or bite to scold you. The dog is in charge. He demands, you obey.

Some dogs are only picky about certain issues. They desire to be in control only in particular situations. For example, there are dogs that only want to be in control of the edible resources. They will try to boss you around and get their way only when food is involved. If you allow the dog to have his way, then he succeeds in being in control. And again, the dog does not act aggressive 100% of the time around food. This type of behavior baffles you because it seems unpredictable. If your dog really believes that he is in charge of the resources and you try to punish him for acting aggressive over food, a confrontation will result. Most likely you will be the one who backs off causing your dog to become even more aggressive. If the highway patrol pulls you over for speeding and you immediately start reprimanding or scolding the officer for giving you a ticket, what do you think his attitude towards your insubordination will be? It is not appropriate to be so disrespectful towards authority. If your dog thinks he is in charge of the situation and you resist, you will pay for your recalcitrance.

The Mean and Nasty Dog

This dog is not much different from the spoiled rotten dog. The dog's attitude of being in charge is the same, it just arrived another way. You didn't spoil and indulge your dog out of misguided love and affection. The dog learned he can control you because you simply let him control you. You were too lazy to do anything differently and you took the path of least resistance. If the dog wants it, give it to him. If the dog won't come when called, don't worry about it. It's too much trouble to obedience train the dog. It's too much trouble doing the confidence building exercises. If the dog doesn't want to be touched, don't bother with it. After all, it's just a dog.

Others of you get to this point because you are afraid of your dog. He growls once and you back away. You don't want the dog to growl again, so whatever you did to make him growl, you avoid. The dog has learned that he can growl and get his way anytime he wants because he knows he can control you. For the first few months or years, everything seemed fine. You knew to never bother the dog while he was eating so any aggressive incident was easy to avoid. Then one day the dog decides he doesn't want to be bothered while sleeping. He growls, you back off and now you don't bother the dog while he is sleeping. Then the dog doesn't want to be touched and so on.

Dominance

The two dogs just described display dominant behavior. "Dominance" is just a fancy way of saying that the dog thinks he's in charge. The dog may indeed be a pushy, confident individual. However, most of the time when the dog is in charge, it's because the dog regards the owner as a weak, untrustworthy, unreliable, inconsistent, undependable push-over. The dog is right. The dog takes control because the owner does not.

Dogs need leadership and if none is provided, they will usually take that position on themselves. We must remember that dogs are pack animals. They are still functioning on a survival level. A pack cannot function and survive without a leader. The dog cannot survive as an individual if the pack does not survive as a group. An instinctive survival need forces the dog to take on a leadership role. The dog may not even want to be the leader but it does so out of perceived necessity. A pushy dog would probably enjoy and gladly take the leadership role.

A top dog or leader doesn't mean that the dog is an aggressive bully. It just means that he has special rights and privileges that come with the position. A top dog can control anything - possessions, resources, location, activity. Just because they can, doesn't mean they do. Just because your Camero can do 120 mph doesn't mean you always go around driving at that speed. You only display your aggressive speeding behavior when you feel like it, or if you are challenged by the driver of a Mustang.

Top dogs are usually kind, affectionate and benevolent. They give and they share. But they are still in charge. They can control the other pack members with a simple glance, a stare, a growl, a showing of teeth, or body posture. They don't rule by force or violence. They don't attack, fight or bite pack members unless challenged or if a subordinate is disrespectful. Since your dog lives with you, you are regarded as part of his pack. If your dog thinks he's top dog, this will explain his apparently contradictory behavior. One moment the dog wants and craves your affection and attention. The next moment, the dog is snarling and snapping. You have over-stepped your boundary. You are acting disrespectful or are challenging the top dog. So the dog growls or snaps at you to scold you and remind you of your place.

Even if you don't out and out spoil your dog, you may still give your dog subtle and sometimes blatant messages that he is indeed top dog. It may be something as simple as the dog nudging you to be petted. He is demanding your attention and you show obedience every time you give in and pet your dog. The dog speaks and you obey. Every time the dog goes to the door and barks or paws to be let outside and again to be let back inside, the dog is in essence demanding that you be his servant. The dog is saying, "Let me out!" or "Let me in!" Leaving food out all day for your dog to nibble on whenever he wants, reinforces in his mind that he has control over the resources. This is a top dog privilege. Every time the dog snaps at you and you withdraw, the dog has said, "Stop that!" and you have obeyed.

Role Reversal

This is one of the most difficult programs for owners to follow. Those who persevere are usually very successful in curing their dog's aggressive behavior.

Changing Your Attitude

Before you can take control of your dog, you must take control of yourself. You must be willing to respect your dog as a dog. You must stop assigning human values and emotions to him. You must stop thinking that your dog does something out of spite, malice, vindictiveness, jealousy or revenge. You must stop treating him like a helpless, human infant. You must gain your dog's trust, respect and confidence.

If you have been unfair or abusive, you must immediately change your ways. Inappropriate punishment is abusive. Never hit, kick, slap or strike your dog with anything. Never reprimand your dog after the fact. You must be consistent. Don't confuse your dog by sometimes allowing disobedience and disrespect and then other times reprimanding him for the same thing. If you ask your dog to do something, don't let the dog learn that you can be ignored. Don't demand obedience and then allow disobedience. This is unfair, inconsistent and only confuses the dog.

If you are truly afraid of the dog, the dog will know it. You cannot be a successful leader if you are frightened of your own dog. If you are not afraid of the dog, but the dog is afraid of you, then you need to go back and build the dog's trust and confidence in you. Without trust and confidence on the part of the dog, you will never be a good leader.

Changing the Dog's Attitude

If your dog thinks he is the leader, then it is high time to dethrone him. You are not going to overthrow his authority by violence or aggression. Remember that pack leaders are gentle, affectionate, trustworthy and consistent. You can establish yourself as the new leader by simple, subtle and effective means. If you feel sorry for the dog and cannot go through with it, then either ·you will have to live with the monster you created or take the chance that someday he will go to the equivalent of the doggy gas chamber for biting.

Start out by simply pulling the royal rug out from under your dog's feet. Reduce "His Majesty" or "Her Highness," to status "Pauper Pup," by immediately taking away all, yes all, rights, privileges, freedoms, enjoyments, luxuries, assets, etc. Take away all toys. All walks, runs, games, play sessions, rides in the car, etc. are immediately terminated. No treats. No free run. The dog door is temporarily sealed. When you are not home, the dog is confined to a small area such as a pen, garage, kitchen, dog-run or crate. When you are home, the dog is on-leash at all times. Either tie the other end of the leash to a heavy piece of furniture or to yourself so the dog has no freedom to even walk around in his former kingdom. Never leave the dog tied down unattended, lest he tangle and injure himself. Do not allow the dog on any furniture. The dog must sleep on the floor, in a crate or in his confinement area (pen, run, etc.). The dog is not allowed in your bedroom. Do not talk to, look at or touch the dog. No hugging, cuddling, petting, snuggling. Do not touch the dog except out of absolute necessity, such as to put on a leash or take it off. The dog is taken out only for official toilet business. Offer food twice a day and hand-feed the dog. If the dog eats, fine. If not, no more food is offered until the next regularly scheduled mealtime. The dog does not have ready access to water except when you are not home. When you are home, the dog is only allowed water when you offer it. Offer water every couple of hours. Remember to take the dog out to urinate shortly after he drinks. In other words, only tend to the dog's basic physical survival needs.

Continue with this deprivation (typically 10 days to three weeks) until you notice a remarkable change in your dog's attitude. Your dog will no longer feel in control and in charge. Suddenly the dog will realize that he needs you after all.

Now it's time for obedience training. At a minimum, train your dog to come, sit, lie down, stay and heel. Reintroduce all of life's luxuries, but via courtesy of you, the new leader. For example, before petting or talking to the dog, he must down stay for 5 minutes. While preparing the dog's food, make him down stay. Before giving the food, the dog must come and sit, then stay until you say it's okay to start eating. Before throwing a ball, the dog must sit. No sit, no play. Before, during and after all walks, the dog must practice his obedience. The dog will see all of his former possessions and privileges are provided and dispensed by you.

Your dog must never be allowed to take or demand anything again. By all means, give whatever you want, but on your terms. The dog must always say, "Please and thank you," instead of taking things for granted. How? By obeying a simple obedience command. Your dog gets nothing for free. There is no more nudging, pawing, barking to make you obey. In fact, your dog shows respect for you by complying with your request before receiving anything. This will establish you as top dog, leader and provider in no time. Don't forget that while your dog sees you as provider and leader, he must also trust you. Go back and review how to gain your dog's trust and confidence, plus any other pertinent section such as play biting.

If at any time the dog forgets his place and growls, snarls, snaps or shows any signs of aggression, immediately return to the "deprivation" routine and begin again.

No Cop-Outs

Some of you think that all you have to do is send your dog off to an expensive training camp and your problems will be over. If you are the cause of your dog's problems, having the dog trained by someone else is not going to help you. You are the one who needs to be trained. You are the one who needs to train your own dog. A good dog trainer can train almost any dog. But so what? What good is a dog that is obedient for the dog trainer? Your dog needs to be obedient, confident and respectful of you, the owner, the person who lives with the dog. The dog trainer cannot teach your dog to respect and trust you. You must do that yourself. Sending your problem dog off to be trained is as silly as sending your partner off to the health center so you can lose 20 pounds or so that you can stop smoking.

RANDOM, UNPROVOKED, UNPREDICTABLE AGGRESSION

Chapter 13

Aha! If you immediately flipped to this section, then I've caught you. If you have read the previous chapters on aggression you would already know that aggression is almost never random, unprovoked or unpredictable. No dog acts aggressive all the time. Most dogs are great 99% of the time. If they exhibit aggressive behavior, it is only a minor part of their life. Their aggressive display may be occasional because it's only occasionally that you annoy or frighten the dog causing her to growl or bite. It's only occasionally that you try to take a possession away or touch her feet. The aggression may seem random or unpredictable because it may depend upon how your dog feels at the moment. If the dog is feeling tolerant, she might not mind being touched. But if she doesn't want to be bothered, she might suddenly growl at you for the same touch.

JEKYLL AND HYDE

Chapter 14

Your dog is always learning. Every time you interact with your dog, you are teaching her something. You do this whether you intend to or not. The biggest complaints I hear come from those who have gone out of their way to train their dog to misbehave. Stop for a moment and evaluate your own behavior. What are you telling your dog on a day to day and minute to minute basis?

The average owner does not spend any time formally training their dog. A good owner will go to a training class and practice five minutes a day a few times a week and ten minutes before classtime. After that, training goes to hell in a hand-basket. An exceptional owner will maintain their dog's training by practicing for ten minutes a day. Even if you trained your dog for 45 minutes everyday (and this is highly unlikely), what goes on the other 23 hours and 15 minutes each day? Most owners quickly undo all the training they have done. People always tell me that the dog is wonderfully obedient and well-behaved whenever they are practicing their routines in the home or in class, but the dog will do absolutely nothing when she is distracted.

What they are saying is that they are not practicing the dog's training when and where they need it the most. So what if the dog does a perfect heel, sit, down-stay in the middle of your living room or in the obedience ring? What the owner wants is a dog that will come, stay and heel in the park; when company is at the door; or when a cat is teasing the dog from the fence.

Your dog knows that she doesn't have to obey in these situations. You have trained your dog to obey only during training sessions. If you tell the dog to come or stay in a distracting situation and she doesn't, most of you do absolutely nothing. The dog gets clean away with disobedience. So in effect, you have taught the dog that she need not obey when she doesn't want to. You have no right to get angry at your dog when she knows what "come here" means and fails to comply. You are the one who has taught your dog that it is perfectly okay to ignore you.

Don't get mad at the dog for behavior that you have taught her. Every time you condone, ignore or tolerate misbehavior and disobedience, you are actively teaching your dog to misbehave. Your dog is obediently being disobedient, just as you have trained her.

Following is a classic case of training a dog to be disobedient.

You go to the park with your puppy and she naively comes every time you call. You happily and proudly put the pup on leash and head for home. In a matter of weeks, the pup comes only 90% of the time and you're still happy. That 90% quickly becomes zero because every time the dog doesn't come, she is learning something. She is also learning something when she does come. Everything you do teaches the dog exactly what you don't want. If the dog does come, you "punish" her by putting her on leash and taking her home. The dog was having the time of her life until you ruined it with the phrase "come here." If the dog doesn't come, she rewards herself by prolonging her play time. Your dog has learned that you will call her 297 times and then you will finally come and get her. So why should she bother going to you?

Then one day, you are late for work and you don't have time to call 297 times. You get upset and very angry that the dog won't come. This time when you go to get the dog, in your frustration and lack of control, you scream and smack the dog on her rump with the leash. Now what have you taught the dog? Run away when the owner approaches unless you want to be punished. You and only you have ruined your dog's previously perfect "come here." Unfortunately, in these situations, most owners think their dog is untrainable, untrustworthy, vindictive, evil, spiteful and so on. I've even heard owners say that their dog is stupid.

If your dog could talk, she would say that you are Dr. Jekyll and Mr. Hyde. For the most part you are a loving, affectionate human being. But you also have episodes of unpredictable, violent, unnatural, and aggressive behavior. Are you a product of bad breeding or was it your environment and training? Can you be retrained? Would spanking you or doing an alpha roll-over help? Should you be put up for adoption? No, it would be unethical to give you away to some other unsuspecting canine. Perhaps the most humane thing to do is to have you euthanized.

Is that fair?

No more for you than for the dog. Our dogs' behavior is primarily a result of our interactions with them. If we don't like our dog's behavior, it is usually the result of what we have done or failed to do. If your dog does the wrong thing, then show him how to do the right thing. Set your dog up to succeed. Set yourself up to succeed. Then celebrate your success together. Be patient, but above all else, be consistent.

Help! My Dog Has An Attitude!